"Julie Clawson had me at 'Don't panic.' While many resources on social justice leave even the most compassionate souls and generous hearts frozen with an overwhelming panic from not knowing where to begin, *Everyday Justice* fires readers up and leaves them ready to change the world—starting right in their everyday lives. Clawson's well-researched and well-written book flows with stories of evil and good, monsters and heroes. It's a must-read for anyone who wants a deeper understanding of what loving our neighbors should look like."

Caryn Rivadeneira, managing editor, *Gifted for Leadership*, and author of *Mama's Got a Fake I.D.*

"Living justly is an overwhelming task these days. How do I know whether the coffee I'm drinking was fairly grown? Or whether my jeans were made by a twelve-year-old? It's daunting, and we're tempted toward apathy. That's why Julie Clawson has done us such a service in writing *Everyday Justice*—in readable, compelling prose, she lays out the truth behind some of the products we use every day, and she gives us practical steps for living justly in a consumeristic age. She avoids guilt trips and writes personally. This book is needed and deserves a wide readership."

Tony Jones (www.tonyj.net), author of *The New Christians: Dispatches from the Emergent Frontier*

"Julie Clawson is a significant and much-needed voice in the emerging church conversation—actually, in any faith conversation. For those of us who have long felt her voice needed to be heard, *Everyday Justice* is a cause for celebration. Only someone who lives a life of social integrity is entitled to write such a book, and Julie is that person. She offers us hope that we can all contribute in a meaningful way to the transformation of our culture."

Marcia Ford, author of *We the Purple: Faith, Politics and the Independent Voter*

"When I was a young Christian I was told that our job was to get people to heaven. The world (like now) was a mess, so evacuating people seemed like a good idea. What if instead I had been told that our main job was to bring the kingdom of God to our planet? What if that meant doing very practical things like advocating for people who were poor, voiceless and powerless? And what if I'd been told Jesus will only return when his followers have improved the situation for those people so much that it's finally become habitable for heaven? That's what I think now. If this idea intrigues you, read this book. It provides the how-tos."

Jim Henderson, executive director, Off The Map

"Julie Clawson gets it. First, she gets it that most of us suburban Americans feel overwhelmed and guilty when we hear about justice. That's why she focuses on positive, doable ways that we can improve the justice quotient of our lives. Second, she gets it that we in the 'developed world' often have an undeveloped theology and lifestyle when it comes to key issues like fair trade, modern-day slavery, fossil fuel dependence, ethical eating and buying, and debt. That's why she gently, positively and hopefully helps us get 'development' where we need it most."

Brian McLaren, author/activist (brianmclaren.net)

"With both tenderness and everyday practicality, Julie Clawson invites all of us into a more complete way of following Jesus. By providing simple, concrete ways to seek justice in our daily lives, *Everyday Justice* is a great resource to get you started or keep you going on the journey toward acting justly, loving mercy and walking humbly with your God."

Will Samson, coauthor of *Justice in the Burbs*

Everyday Justice

THE GLOBAL IMPACT OF OUR DAILY CHOICES

JULIE CLAWSON

Foreword by Tom and Christine Sine

IVP Books

An imprint of InterVarsity Press
Downers Grove, Illinois

InterVarsity Press
P.O. Box 1400, Downers Grove, IL 60515-1426
World Wide Web: www.ivpress.com
E-mail: email@ivpress.com

InterVarsity Press® is the book-publishing division of InterVarsity Christian Fellowship/USA®,
a student movement active on campus at hundreds of universities, colleges and schools of nursing in
the United States of America, and a member movement of the International Fellowship of Evangelical
Students. For information about local and regional activities, write Public Relations Dept.,
InterVarsity Christian Fellowship/USA, 6400 Schroeder Rd., P.O. Box 7895, Madison, WI
53707-7895, or visit the IVCF website at <www.intervarsity.org>.

All Scripture quotations, unless otherwise indicated, are taken from the Holy Bible, Today's New
International Version™ Copyright © 2001 by International Bible Society. All rights reserved.

Design: Cindy Kiple

Images: bag of garbage: Stefan Klein/iStockphoto
    cheeseburger: Kelly Cline/iStockphoto
    chocolate bars: Georgina Palmer/iStockphoto
    credit cards: iStockphoto
    disposable coffee cup: Chris Hutchison
    gas pump nozzle: Skip Odonnell
    head of lettuce: Susan Trigg/iStockphoto
    stack of sweaters: iStockphoto

ISBN 978-0-8308-3628-4

Printed in the United States of America ∞

 green press INITIATIVE InterVarsity Press is committed to protecting the environment and to the responsible
use of natural resources. As a member of Green Press Initiative we use recycled paper
whenever possible. To learn more about the Green Press Initiative, visit <www.
greenpressinitiative.org>.

Library of Congress Cataloging-in-Publication Data

Clawson, Julie, 1977-
    Everyday justice: the global impact of our daily choices / Julie
Clawson.
        p. cm.
    Includes bibliographical references.
    ISBN 978-0-8308-3628-4 (pbk.: alk. paper)
    1. Distributive justice—Religious aspects—Christianity. 2.
Christian ethics. I. Title.
    BT738.C545 2009
    241'.622—dc22

                                                                    2009021600

P   22   21   20   19   18   17   16   15   14   13   12   11   10   9   8   7   6   5   4   3   2   1
Y   27   26   25   24   23   22   21   20   19   18   17   16   15   14   13   12   11   10   09

For Via Christus Community Church—
thanks for walking with me on this journey.

Contents

Foreword by Tom and Christine Sine / 9

WARNING! *Read Before Proceeding* / 13

Introduction / 17

1. COFFEE: *Fair Trade and the Daily Latte* / 31

2. CHOCOLATE: *Modern-Day Slavery Exposed* / 53

3. CARS: *The Global and Local Impact of Oil Consumption* / 75

4. FOOD: *Choosing to Eat Ethically* / 95

5. CLOTHES: *The Story Behind What We Wear* / 119

6. WASTE: *The High Price of Our Dirty Little Habits* / 143

7. DEBT: *Proclaiming Jubilee to the Nations* / 165

Conclusion / 185

Acknowledgments / 191

Notes / 193

About the Author / 207

Foreword

In *Everyday Justice* Julie Clawson challenges us to recognize that every choice we make has implications that reverberate around the world. How we dress, what we eat, where we shop are all ethical choices that should be informed and molded by our faith. This is a challenge that we both constantly struggle with as we grapple with how to translate our faith and these implications into tangible, doable actions.

In the midst of our struggle we are challenged by a growing number of young people who, like Julie, are convinced that their faith should impact all these daily decisions. They recognize that at the center of our faith is a God who intends to transform and make new all creation. Our God cares deeply for all the people of the world and challenges us to commit our lives to being a part of that transformation, which means committing ourselves to justice and creation care as a way of life, not just as a theology we salute.

I (Christine) did not grow up in an environment that encouraged me to think about issues of justice. The idea that my everyday choices could have dire consequences for people I have never met and probably never will meet was quite foreign to me. To be honest it did not occur to me that these decisions had anything to do with my faith either until I started traveling in Africa and Asia.

There I met some of the people who grew my coffee beans and sewed my cheap clothes. Suddenly these people had faces—faces marked by suffering and pain because of my indifference. Their starving children were no longer news clips on the eleven o'clock news but children I cared about and longed to see have the same life advantages I take for granted.

It wasn't that I had directly hurt them or their families, but my silence spoke volumes. I started to realize that every time I bought something produced in a sweatshop, my silence meant that I didn't care if the workers were paid unjust wages. Every time I purchased food that had been sprayed with toxic chemicals, my silence spoke of my complicity in environmental pollution. And every time I purchased coffee produced by peasant farmers who received virtually nothing for their long hard labor, I contributed to their poverty and unjust toil.

Part of what Julie does in *Everyday Justice* is what I experienced during my time in Africa and Asia. She makes the people who grow our food and produce our clothes come to life for us. She helps us to see that they too are our neighbors even though they may live on the other side of the world. More than that she enables us to see them as children whom God loves and whom Christ died for. And of course that recognition forces all of us to view our lives and our daily decisions in a different light.

Recognizing the ethical dilemmas of daily life and grappling with these as a part of our life journey is not easy for any of us. It means we have to make hard decisions on a daily basis, which can be overwhelming. Often we feel we don't know where to turn for answers.

Everyday Justice filled us with hope as we read Julie's insights and the practical ideas she shares of how we can make decisions that really will bring everyday justice. These suggestions are possible for all of us to implement without panicking or feeling overwhelmed. They are small ways in which we can all become a part of God's mustard-seed movement that is quietly changing our world.

We invite you to join this exciting journey with followers of Jesus from around the globe and recognize that your life too can make a difference in our troubled world. As we commit ourselves to everyday acts of justice, together we can bring glimpses of God's shalom world of wholeness and abundance into being.

Tom and Christine Sine

Warning!

READ BEFORE PROCEEDING

D_on't panic._ I think any book on living justly needs to have those words displayed prominently across the cover. With respect to Douglas Adams, whose _Hitchhiker's Guide to the Galaxy_ has those very words inscribed in large, friendly letters on the cover, I think those of us exploring how to integrate justice into our lives need a reminder not to panic.

All too often I find that conversations that involve changing our lifestyles result in us feeling overwhelmed at the sheer immensity of the problem. There is too much hurt out there, too much that needs to change, and too much to tackle all at once. From just becoming aware of the needs in the world, to realizing that our lifestyle choices make a difference, to understanding how our faith informs how we approach justice issues, we can feel shaken to the core.

Encountering new ideas and allowing those ideas to change who we are is a huge step for most of us. Too often we live compartmentalized lives that don't allow for the different spheres of our existence to interact. Church is separate from shopping. Our morning latte doesn't connect with our volunteer work (besides giving us a needed caffeine boost). Our waste disposal habits are removed from our politics. They each exist separately and apart in our hectic lives.

But encountering justice issues changes all of that. Our lives are no longer just a series of unrelated tasks and errands with the occasional leisure activity thrown in when there's time. Our lives are part of a bigger picture. Our local, everyday choices reverberate around the world. And at the center, pushing and informing all of those choices, is our faith. Life suddenly becomes a lot more complicated. Acting justly every day means developing awareness about the problems in the world; it means changing how we shop, how we dress and how we drive; it means starting to see our each and every action as an ethical choice.

So you can begin to see why the warning "Don't panic" might be necessary. Making sense of all this stuff, much less actually doing anything about it, seems nearly impossible. Even if we want to jump headfirst into a life of living justly, we may fear that we will drown in the vastness of the problems. We want to change the world, but sometimes it's hard to even know where to begin. We panic, we get overwhelmed, and we let our feelings of inadequacy paralyze us. We see acting justly as an all-or-nothing endeavor, and because we can't do it all, we often end up doing nothing.

This book exists to help us start doing something by giving concrete and practical steps to help us live justly in the everyday. I fully admit to the enormity of the problems, which are often too much for one person to fully grasp. The pain and suffering in this world are immense, as are the many systemic injustices that perpetuate cultures of poverty and oppression. I will explore some of the stories of ways systemic injustices are played out in people's lives and then examine ways that our lifestyle choices exacerbate the problems. This may shock and overwhelm you at times, but the point is not to leave you feeling guilty and helpless. This book tells the intricate and complicated stories of injustice for specific reasons: (1) so we can see how our Christian faith should inform our response to those issues and (2) so we can discover practical ways we can start working for justice in our day-to-day lives.

To change the world, we must start somewhere. It can be easy to sign a petition, wear a bracelet, put a banner on our blog or a bumper sticker on our car, or simply give money to help with a cause, but to really start effecting change we have to actually start tweaking the way we live.

And yes, I said tweak—not overhaul.

Asking people to completely overhaul their lives after reading a book is unrealistic. Such a request prompts the feelings of panic I mentioned before. A few of us *might* be ready for the overhaul, but we are *all* capable of tweaking. All of us can discern where God is leading us to alter our lives—to change one thing at a time, taking the time to really understand and get behind our actions. Sometimes insisting that the revolution be slow means that it will actually be *doable*.

I like the approach Benjamin Franklin took to becoming a virtuous person. Somewhat tongue-in-cheek, Franklin "conceiv'd the bold and arduous Project of arriving at moral Perfection."[1] He then compiled a list of thirteen virtues he desired to incorporate into his life. Discovering he "had undertaken a Task of more Difficulty than [he] had imagined,"[2] he decided against vowing to start living completely virtuously immediately (as many of us do every New Year's Day). Instead he decided to tackle one virtue a week as he worked his way to his desired state of perfection. Using an eighteenth-century, pen-and-paper spreadsheet to keep track of his progress, he embarked on the quest for virtue. He, of course, discovered that he had many more faults than he expected, but over time, he had the pleasure of watching those faults diminish as virtue increased.

Those of us seeking to live justly wouldn't be amiss to follow Franklin's example. One thing at a time. Slow, step-by-step changes in our lives. This book presents sometimes-overwhelming amounts of information, yet this book hardly scratches the surface of many of the issues. The point is not to force change on

people or to expect everyone's journey into everyday justice to
look the same. This book is a starting line. I hope it will provide
some helpful information to acquaint you with the nature of the
conversation and provide some good ideas on how to respond.
But you need to take it at your own pace. Research the issues that
strike you; go deeper on those that touch your heart. Explore
more on what the Bible has to say about justice. Try a new type
of food. Watch a documentary. Shop at a different store. Do what
you can when you can.

And like I said: just don't panic.

Introduction

The Spirit of the Lord is on me,
   because he has anointed me
   to proclaim good news to the poor.
He has sent me to proclaim freedom for the prisoners
   and recovery of sight for the blind,
to set the oppressed free,
   to proclaim the year of the Lord's favor. (Lk 4:18-19)

Jesus came to loose the chains of injustice. He came to set the captives free. The book of Luke records that, at the inauguration of his public ministry, Jesus stood up and read those words from the scroll of Isaiah. Luke then writes:

[Jesus] rolled up the scroll, gave it back to the attendant and sat down. The eyes of everyone in the synagogue were fastened on him. He began by saying to them, "Today this scripture is fulfilled in your hearing." (Lk 4:20-21)

Jesus knew his people lived under oppression. The Roman military government controlled them and occupied their land. Jesus offered a way of peace and love even amidst their lack of freedom. He knew his people needed change—a revolution to establish a new way of living. But in his typical upside-down fashion, he proposed a revolution more radical than any violent uprising, more subversive than any secret army: a revolution of justice guided by his principles of compassion and love.

Most of us know that Jesus suffered and died to set us free from the power of sin, but that is only part of the gospel story. His mission and message actually extend far beyond that. By setting people free from the oppression of sin within us, Jesus enables us to live differently from the oppressive and unjust systems of the world around us as well. His life, death and resurrection inaugurated a new kingdom, and he taught his disciples to live according to the revolutionary values of this kingdom of God: to care for the needy, to treat one's enemies with love, to feed the hungry, to work for justice. And then he told them to go and make more disciples, "teaching them to obey everything I have commanded you" (Mt 28:20). Jesus wanted this peaceful revolution, his kingdom of justice and love, to spread.

I believe the way of justice that Jesus demonstrated and called us to live is possible. I believe we can live out love and peace and justice in our day-to-day lives. But I rarely see it happening around me—in the world or in the church. Sure, there are pockets of it, communities here and there that promote justice, but working for justice is not a widespread spiritual practice in many churches. I've yet to witness the revolution Jesus came to start—which is why I work toward it myself.

With God's help, as much as I can, I seek to live justly. But I didn't always care about justice or understand how my everyday actions affected the world around me. Justice wasn't brought up much in the churches I attended, so it took digging deep into the Bible myself before I realized that living justly is a major part of what God asks of his followers.

In a chapel session during my freshman year at Wheaton College, I was introduced to the global impact of my daily choices.

The speaker detailed how major soft drink companies contributed to the genocide in Darfur as they sought to protect their trade sources above all else.[1] The information shocked me, having never considered that what I chose to fill my cup with in the cafeteria had implications for people halfway around the globe. That was my first wake-up call, and since then, I have been discovering how important to my faith it is to live justly.

Choosing to follow Jesus is more than just adhering to a set of beliefs; it is an invitation into an entirely new way of living in the world. We're not called to merely sit around and wait for heaven after we die. Rather we are called to help God's kingdom come and his will be done "on earth as it is in heaven." The life he calls us to involves walking with Jesus and carrying the cross with him, caring for the things he cared about: Seeking justice. Rescuing the oppressed. Living a life of love and peace. Understanding this has been a journey for me, and as I work for justice, I hope to encourage others to join me along the way.

Living justly is not only possible, it's necessary today more than ever. Injustices abound in this hurting world, but Jesus calls his church to do something about it. This book is about "doing something." Sometimes, with all the celebrity hype around justice issues, it is hard to understand what Christians are called to actually do, and it is even harder to grasp tangible ways to do whatever that is. This book provides an overview of what the Bible says about justice, what current justice-needs exist in the world today and what exactly we can do about them. It won't answer every question or explore every detail, but I hope it will help you gain a better understanding of what God's mandate to "act justly" means in your life.

But first I think we need to back up a step and define what this word *justice* is all about.

UNDERSTANDING JUSTICE

Defining justice can be a bit slippery. I've heard it defined as "equality and fairness," "common decency" or "enforcing laws." The dictionary isn't much help either with its definition: "to act or treat justly."[2] (I thought you weren't supposed to use the word in the definition!) While all of these definitions hint at what biblical justice is all about, they don't quite present the full picture.

Justice, at its very core, deals with relationships—our relationships to God, to each other and to the world. The Bible tells us that we are made in the image of God (Gen 1:27), implying that we, in a sense, represent God to the world. This responsibility of bearing God's image ought to define our relationships, as we are to reflect God's image to each other and have that image reflect back to God in everything that we do. And if God's character is love, as we are told in 1 John 4:16, then to reflect God's image is to reflect love to others in the form of care, compassion and concern for their well-being. To act justly, then, is to represent God's love to each other and thereby honor the image of God in the other person as well.

But because of sin, our relationships are broken and in need of healing. Whether we intend to or not, our everyday actions hurt others and damage those relationships. Through anger and malice, self-centeredness and greed, we deny the image of God in others and fail to reflect God's love to them. We treat others unfairly or unequally, using them as objects that can be exploited for personal gain. We oppress them, torture them and kill them—or simply ignore them—instead of seeing them as our brothers and sisters, created in the image of God, just like us. In other words, we treat them with injustice. This results in what theologian Scot McKnight calls "cracked eikons"—broken reflections of the image of God.[3]

These are hard words, and they probably seem distant from the day-to-day reality of our lives. Most of us can't recall ever killing a person, but this book will explore the ways we often unwittingly participate in these injustices. The purpose is not to make us feel guilty but to help us stop and seek justice instead. What is obvious is that we live in a world full of brokenness. Damaged relationships lay strewn about us and the longing to be healed and whole is unshakable. We want a better world—a world without the brokenness.

But we aren't without hope. Through his life, death and resurrection, Jesus made possible the healing and the restoration of our relationships. Jesus offers forgiveness to each of us and provides us with the strength to extend that forgiveness to others. Through him, our brokenness and damaged relationships can begin to heal. Choosing to accept that healing is choosing to join Jesus in his mission of restoring the image of God in people. Jesus called us to serve as his hands and feet by helping to restore relationships through acts of justice, which flow from our love for God and love for others.

Justice can thus be defined simply as the practical outworking of loving God and others. Or as Dr. Cornel West puts it, "justice is what love looks like in public."[4] Jesus tells us that the greatest commandments are to "'Love the Lord your God with all your heart and with all your soul and with all your strength and with all your mind'; and, 'Love your neighbor as yourself'" (Lk 10:27).

JUSTICE: the practical result of loving God and loving others.

These commands cover all of our relationships. When we choose to love God and love others, we have no choice but to treat others with respect and fairness as we acknowledge them as fellow image-bearers. We have to treat them as we ourselves desire to be treated and act in ways that show concern for their welfare. In other words, if we are to truly live out the command to love then we have to act justly.

But this definition doesn't represent the way most of us typically speak of justice. So let's expand this understanding a bit and explore a common conception of justice in light of this biblical understanding of justice.

Justice as punishment versus justice as restoration. The familiar phrase "making sure justice is served" better represents the common conception of justice. In this phrase, *justice* refers to "punishment for wrongdoing" (e.g., a criminal commits a crime and must pay the consequences). We speak of the Department of Justice, justices of the peace or even that famous band of superheroes, the Justice League. These groups make sure the laws of society are followed . . . or else. That "or else" implies that the people who make up those groups will inflict *justice,* meaning "punishment," on those who transgress.

However, justice in the biblical sense, as used above, carries a much deeper meaning than mere punishment—a meaning that includes healing and restoration as well. In punishing criminals, we hope that they will eventually be restored, so they can then go and live rightly. *Justice,* in its most basic sense in the English language, implies living righteously: being morally right, equitable, fair. One of the earliest recorded usages of the concept in Old English was when the term *rehtwisnisse* ("righteousness") was used as a translation of the Latin term *justitia* ("justice").[5] In addition, the most common Hebrew, *tsedeq,* and Greek, *dikaios,* words for these concepts are alternately translated in English as both "righteousness" and "justice." To live righteously is to live justly; they are one and the same.

The public versus private distinctions implied in our modern understanding of *righteousness* and *justice* didn't exist during biblical times. In other words, righteousness is more than just personal piety or private moral character; it has both individual and social implications. It involves our relationship with God and with others, following the call to love them as we love ourselves. Loving others by seeking what is right, good and fair for them is not only how we act justly, it is also how we live righteously.

Justice then becomes much more than simply a punishment for wrongdoing. Instead of only punishing wrongdoers in the hope that they will then live rightly, biblical justice involves healing the brokenness that marred our relationships with each other in the first place. Justice, in this sense, involves restoring broken relationships between people, and putting right all the ways sin and injustice harm ourselves, each other and the world. No doubt putting right the wrongs will sometimes require punishing the wrongdoers—to prevent them from continuing in their injustices and, perhaps, to make them aware of the seriousness of their actions. But a fuller application of justice would actually be to restore the wrongdoers to whole and healed relationships as well. If we respect the image of God in *all* people, then we need to not only heal the ways that image has been marred in the victims of injustice, we need to also heal the ways the image of God is marred in the perpetrators of injustice.

The true practice of justice thus moves away from retribution (punishment) and toward restoration. We restore broken relationships, we restore families torn asunder, and we even restore damaged land so that life may survive and flourish. To live justly in our own lives means living so that this restoration can happen. *Justice,* understood exclusively in terms of punishment, involves tearing people down, but *justice,* understood as righteousness and restoration, results in helping people rebuild—both perpetrators and victims.

For instance, we can prosecute and punish those who engage in human sex trafficking, but true justice doesn't stop there. Truly restorative justice must also involve helping the women and children who are victims of this evil to regain their lives and their dignity, and it could even involve bringing the traffickers to a point of genuine remorse and repentance for their evil—so they too could eventually be restored as the whole and healed people God created them to be.

Or, to take another example, if we act justly so that poor farmers receive a fair wage for the work they do, then their lives will be restored. They will have money to buy food and send their children to school, and their dignity as human beings who are treated with respect and fairness will be reestablished. Justice, in this case, has nothing to do with punishment and everything to do with restoration.

This restoration is what the Bible says is happening when justice gets lived out. I love how *The Message* version of the Bible translates Isaiah 58:9-12:

> If you get rid of unfair practices,
>   quit blaming victims,
>   quit gossiping about other people's sins,
> If you are generous with the hungry
>   and start giving yourselves to the down-and-out,
> Your lives will begin to glow in the darkness,
>   your shadowed lives will be bathed in sunlight.
> I will always show you where to go.
>   I'll give you a full life in the emptiest of places—
>   firm muscles, strong bones.
> You'll be like a well-watered garden,
>   a gurgling spring that never runs dry.
> You'll use the old rubble of past lives to build anew,
>   rebuild the foundations from out of your past.
> You'll be known as those who can fix anything,
>   restore old ruins, rebuild and renovate,
>   make the community livable again.

Choosing to live justly—getting rid of unfair practices and, for example, being generous with the hungry—results in restoration and healing. It is a beautiful outpouring of the way God intends us to live. If we engage in right living (righteousness) by acting justly, we will help provide a just way of life for others. We will help make our communities, and the community of the whole world, livable again.

SO WHAT DOES THIS CALL TO JUSTICE INVOLVE?

It sounds great to talk about restoring broken relationships and healing the world, but it's a tad harder to figure out exactly how to go about doing so. It may be easy to see that people are hungry, but seeing how we deny the image of God in others is a bit more difficult. We may not tend to think that the ways we live our everyday lives have much effect on the lives of others, but our circle of influence is actually much larger than we think.

The youth pastor I had as a teenager liked the statement, "Every decision has a price tag." I think he intended it to scare us away from behaviors like premarital sex and drinking, but I believe its application can go much further. Every decision we make does carry a price, but that price is often paid by the people whose lives are affected by our actions. Every decision we make is an ethical decision, which forces us to choose whether we will act out of love or end up denying the image of God in others.

For example, that banana my daughter ate for breakfast this morning involved an ethical decision. By buying and eating that banana, I support everything that banana represents. If that banana was grown by farmers who were kept in near-slavelike conditions, paid pennies a day, exposed to hazardous chemicals and beaten by hired terrorists if they protested their work conditions, I am supporting those things.

Or how about my T-shirt? If a fourteen-year-old girl, who is forced to work in a factory because her parents owe money to the owner (money they borrowed to pay for medical bills), made my T-shirt, and she is paid, maybe, five cents a shirt (that I paid $19.99 for) by the owner who also forces her to sleep with him in order to keep her job, then I am supporting her exploitation and rape.

Don't get me wrong: I know no one reading this book consciously supports slavery, terrorism, exploitation or rape. But we vote with our money, spent on such bananas or T-shirts, and we make the ethical decision to support those very things whether we intend to or not. We effectively deny the image of God in those workers by telling them that our shopping habits and consumer needs are more important than their dignity of life. The cost they are paying is the price tag of our decisions.

Living justly means understanding the impact of our decisions. It involves not only an awareness of the needs of others but also choosing to love others in a way that cares for their needs. It forces us to take a hard look at how our everyday choices (what we wear, what we eat, what we drive, etc.) affect others. An important aspect of acting justly is to first stop being complicit in injustice. As the Isaiah passage mentions, the justice God wants from us involves being "generous with the hungry," but also getting "rid of unfair practices." We will still need to be consumers, but instead of becoming complicit in injustice, we can promote ethical consumption. Ethical consumption implies that we will apply our moral values and ethical standards to our consumer habits. We don't opt out of a necessary system, but we attempt to redeem it as we live by a more consistent ethic.

ETHICAL CONSUMPTION:

the application of our moral

values and ethical standards

to our consumer habits.

But justice is complicated. Sometimes it is hard to know how our decisions affect others, and it is even harder to discover loving alternatives. To make things worse, acting justly involves some serious lifestyle changes that can be really difficult. That's okay. The point isn't to instantly create a perfectly just world with the wave of some magic wand. Justice is a journey that is different for every person, and it proceeds at differing speeds. There is no need to get overwhelmed. If we each start small and promote justice where we can, when we can, that marks the beginning of the revolution of love. All we have to do is take that first step into the call that Jesus gave us to love others. And then take the next, and the next, and the next . . .

JUSTICE IS FOR EVERYONE

Churches often talk about our different callings or giftings. Some are called to be teachers, others to be evangelists, etc., but of course, no one person is expected to do it all. But justice is different. Just as we wouldn't say that some are called to be righteous while others are not, we can't say that justice is reserved for a select few either. Justice isn't something to regulate to a committee or talk about once a year. It isn't something for just the young or the old, or for just the super-committed or super-mature believers. Justice, in all its various forms, is for everyone. We might each live it out differently, but God expects us all to seek justice.

The Bible records that God has shown us what he requires of us, which is to act justly, love mercy and to walk humbly with God (Mic 6:8). God wants us to be known as people who love justice, and to even boast that we follow a God who loves justice. In Jeremiah 9:23-24 we read,

This is what the LORD says:

"Let not the wise boast of their wisdom
    or the strong boast of their strength
    or the rich boast of their riches,
but let those who boast boast about this:
    that they understand and know me,
that I am the LORD, who exercises kindness,
    justice and righteousness on earth,
    for in these I delight,"
        declares the LORD.

God delights in justice and desires for us, for all of us, to delight in it as well. Unfortunately recent discussions in the church have left many believing that justice issues are only for certain types of churches or certain political parties. The call to act justly often gets lost in dichotomizing dialogues and misunderstandings. The height of these tensions—the conservative-liberal divide—sadly causes discussions about justice to be tainted with those polarized extremes. For example, if a liberal group talks about caring for the environment, then that must be a liberal issue and, therefore, taboo for good conservatives. Similarly if a conservative group rallies to reduce abortions then that becomes solely a conservative issue.

The problem with this sort of labeling is that it undermines productive dialogue, and it stands in the way of making any real progress or accomplishing true justice. By shuffling justice issues into the conservative and liberal camps we decide that the issues promoted by people different than us are, at best, not important, and at worst, representative of all the bad things we don't like about the other side. We can't see past the labels and actually look for the truth in what others are saying, and thus we risk ignoring justice issues that God would have us care about.

Furthermore, when we start labeling according to us-versus-them categories, we blind ourselves to the human reality of the issues. We forget who we are seeking justice for as we get entrenched in our own ideology. People living in poverty and oppression should not be dismissed as merely a liberal or a conservative issue. They are hungry and exploited. God created them in his image and we are to love them. Not just some of us, either. All of us.

When Jesus said in Matthew 25:35, "For I was hungry and you gave me something to eat," he didn't add the disclaimer "when it agreed with your political agenda." No, Jesus told us to feed the hungry. Period. That's regardless of our (or their) political persuasion. God is bigger than twenty-first-century American politics.

And while it's okay to have political convictions, they shouldn't stand in the way of the call to act justly.

I hope this book will stretch you to take off the liberal or conservative lens and see the world differently. The call to self-sacrificial love should always supersede whatever is written on our voter registration cards. If you thought some justice issues were only issues for *them* to care about, I hope this book can demonstrate that all followers of Christ should care about justice issues wherever they arise.

LET'S DIVE IN

This book exists as a resource and a guide to acting justly. In it you will find discussions of everyday justice issues, biblical guidelines for interacting with those issues and practical steps for acting justly in those areas. Some things might be shocking and new to you, while others may reflect how you are already living and loving others. I hope that everyone can find some help in his or her justice journey within these pages, but don't feel pressured into doing everything—or limited into doing only the things listed here. This is a place to start, not the final (or only) word on living justly.

To help paint the picture of how justice touches our day-to-day lives, I'll start each chapter with brief vignettes that focus on everyday people encountering justice issues. Each of these people knows something about justice issues but not enough to know what to do about them. Often the thought of fitting justice into an already-busy schedule overwhelms them. Their responses, questions and even excuses echo the sentiments expressed by many regarding justice issues.

From there, I'll address the issues these people have encountered and explore how they can alter their lifestyles to pursue justice in a particular area. I'll also tell stories from around the world that put faces on these issues and remind us that our choices affect real people. We'll dig even deeper as we explore what the Bible has to say about justice, and for each issue we look at, I'll include concrete steps that we can take to live justly. If you want additional information about a particular topic, at the end of every chapter is a list of resources you can delve into to discover more.[6] Learning how to act justly every day is an ongoing process, and I hope that these resources will help you proceed in that journey.

God loves justice and calls us to share that love as well. Let's dive into the life God wants us to live and start acting justly.

Coffee

FAIR TRADE AND THE DAILY LATTE

Mark glanced at his watch. Although he was running a few minutes late, he figured he still had time for his morning ritual: a cup of coffee at the corner coffee chain. As he parked his car and headed inside, he wondered what today's trivia question would be. Even with just a ten-cent discount on the line, answering the store's daily trivia question had become a minor obsession for Mark. So he smiled as he wondered what sort of arcane lore he would have to rack his brain for today.

He barely glanced at the college student behind the counter as he ordered his regular—medium, skim latte, extra hot—and read the question of the day posted on a blackboard behind her. "What is the name of our new line of coffee that is sustainably grown and whose production guarantees the growers are paid fair wages?"

Mark rolled his eyes as he remembered the huge display at the front of the store.

"The Fair Trade Jungle Blend," he said to the barista.

She gave him a quizzical look.

"The answer to the trivia question," he prompted.

"Oh, yeah. You're right. Sorry. No one else has bothered answering that yet today. You get the discount."

As he took out his wallet to pay, Mark asked, "So if this is a new line of coffee, does that mean that the rest of the coffee you serve here isn't sustainably produced or doesn't pay the workers fair wages?"

The barista gave him a confused look and shrugged. "I'm not sure what you mean. You can take the flier about the Jungle Blend; I'm sure it will explain all about it. I just sell the stuff. . . . That will be $3.45."

Aware of the growing line behind him, Mark quickly paid for his coffee. He spared a brief glance at the Jungle Blend display as he left, noticing the poster of the smiling Latin American farmers standing under a canopy of trees. Happy workers growing coffee with traditional methods that cared for the land. *It all seems rather idyllic,* he thought as he walked out to his car, *the way I've always thought coffee has been grown.* As he took a sip of his latte, it troubled him a little; he wondered why the store needed to advertise that one of their lines of coffee brought a fair wage to its growers. He knew enough about business to know that highlighting something like that meant that it was special and different. But since when did paying people fairly for their work become the exception not the norm?

It was a disturbing question but one Mark didn't have time for. He was already running late for work and the day promised to be rather busy. So pushing thoughts of fair wages aside, he drove out of the parking lot and took another sip of his latte.

☛

My first introduction to the concept of ethical consumption came through coffee. I was in high school and college during that period in the 1990s when the coffee craze swept the nation. Any and everything related to coffee automatically attained the status of "cool." Gatherings with friends involved hitting the latest new coffee shop—even if a person didn't drink or even like coffee. Like Mark in the story above, I had my latte addiction (and was a tad obsessed with always answering the daily trivia question correctly).

The coolness factor of coffee seeped into the church as well. Serving lattes and flavored cappuccinos (as opposed to the typical churchy offering of slightly burnt, overly percolated, tinted water) became synonymous with "hip" and "relevant" new worship trends. (The "coffee and candles" cliché about the emerging church had to start somewhere, right?) Coffee conveyed status, and for a time, I bought into this trend too. Coffee became more than just the source of beloved caffeine; it represented something bigger than itself, a symbol of the cultural story I wanted to inhabit. Yet for all my flirting with the idea of coffee, it was years before I became aware of the larger story of coffee—a story in which I was an unknowing participant, the story of coffee's origins and the people who produced it for my consumption. Once I encountered that story, I began to see how my coffee-buying habits were actually ethical actions. And that, to use the cliché, is what changed everything.

THE COFFEE STORY

In the world today an estimated twenty-five million people make their living growing coffee.[1] To these farmers coffee is much more than a cultural trend or a status symbol; it is their livelihood. Unfortunately, many of these farmers barely make a living—despite devoting their lives to growing coffee. As many of us make a social habit of dropping four dollars for a cup of coffee, the typical farmer sees little or none of that money. To complicate matters, as the popularity of coffee exploded, the price per pound of coffee paid to the growers plummeted.

Prior to 1989, Western nations abided by the International Coffee Agreement, which held steady the price per pound of coffee.[2] This agreement was a product of the Cold War and was based on the assumption that, if coffee growers received a decent wage, the cultural instability that the communists might take advantage of would never develop. At the same time, as the trendiness of coffee increased (in what the media often refer to as the "Starbucksification" of America), demand for one of the world's already largest commodities grew, and international banking organizations encouraged developing countries to produce more coffee to meet that demand which, predictably, resulted in a surplus of supply. With the end of the Cold War, the United States abandoned the International Coffee Agreement, and the twin effects of supply surplus and loss of government protection sent prices plummeting. So while many farmers toiled full time, they didn't have enough money to feed, house or educate their families.

For instance, Tatu Museyni, a widow and small coffee farmer in Tanzania, recently saw a return of fifteen dollars for her entire yearly crop. She knows that education would provide a better life for her children, but with annual school fees running an average of ten dollars per child, this poor return makes it impossible for her to afford to send her children to school. To merely survive and pay basic medical bills, she must sell even the food she grew for her children to eat, and she has to spend more time away from her six kids by working odd jobs. She laments, "Education is very important. It will help my children to have a better life. That is why I struggle so hard to find the money they need to go to school."[3] She and her children are part of the story about the coffee we drink, and they are suffering because of it.

Farmers like Tatu Museyni, desperate to make any money at all, had to sell the fruits of their labor at prices far below the cost of production. They had no choice except to keep producing their crop and trying to survive. In fact, many of them were locked into growing coffee by government mandates or lived on land where the soil and terrain limited their crop options. Options didn't really exist for them. But in a broken economic system, their well-being mattered far less than profit for others.

The five companies (Nestlé, Kraft, Procter & Gamble, Sara Lee and the German Tchibo) that control 50 percent of the global coffee market set the demand and determine the prices.[4] They are the ones who choose how much coffee to buy and what they will pay for that coffee. Smaller companies look to the standards the big companies set when they go to buy coffee. After years of falling prices, the market hit an all-time low in 2001, devastating the lives of coffee growers around the world. While the farmers struggled to survive, consumers in 2001 didn't see a drop in the price of their lattes. Instead the coffee production companies saw a huge increase in their profits.

While making a profit is the basic goal of most companies, the question arises whether making a profit justifies the ongoing harm done to coffee growers around the world, forcing hard-working farmers deeper and deeper into poverty. This is the system that we, as consumers, support each time we spend our money on coffee, and this is where economics and ethics start to collide. Numbers and statistics about supply and demand can tell part of the story, but to fully understand the immensity of the problem, we need to see the effects on the lives of real people.

THE COFFEE FARMERS

The coffee crisis directly affected Lawrence Seguya, a Ugandan coffee farmer. He wishes that Western coffee consumers understood "that the drink they are enjoying is the cause of all our problems. We grow it with our sweat and sell it for nothing."[5] Coffee growers around the world echo his sentiment. Coffee continues to sell for less than the cost of production. In some areas of Vietnam, coffee sells for merely 60 percent of what it costs to produce.[6] And in areas of Mexico, the farmer can often see a return of less than a third of his production costs, leaving him with an annual income of less than six hundred dollars.[7] While that amount hardly covers the annual cost of a daily latte habit, these farmers must struggle to simply survive on that income.

After years of taking a loss on their crop, the farmers face tough choices. Without income, families must cut back on food and basic medicines, as well as cut other corners wherever possible. For many this means that children, especially the girls, must be withdrawn from school, since in most countries, there is no such thing as free public education.[8] As the cycles of poverty and debt increase, farmers eventually end up losing their land and must go looking for work elsewhere.

The typical first resort for these farmers is to move into the already overcrowded cities where jobs are scarce. In Mexico this is the common plight of coffee farmers and others who've seen their livelihoods undermined and lives ruined by "free" trade and the influx of tariff-free, subsidized U.S. goods. While in theory, free trade is good for all, in reality there is nowhere in the world where free trade actually exists. Instead, unequal trade agreements mean that someone, generally the poor and powerless, suffers while others prosper. When governments subsidize crops it is meant to help out farmers, but issues arise when subsidized goods (which can sell at lower prices because of the subsidies) come into direct competition with unsubsidized goods. So, for instance, when the North American Free Trade Agreement (NAFTA) allowed subsidized U.S. goods that were not being subjected to an additional tariff to flood the Mexican market, many Mexican farmers could no longer afford to compete. They often lost their farms as the price awarded their labors steadily dropped.[9] Shantytowns sprung up on the outskirts of Mexico City, full of farmers no longer able to survive in what, usually, had been their family's profession for centuries. Yet there are only so many jobs available in the cities, so to feed their families, some displaced farmers consider last-resort options: start growing well-paying (but illegal) crops or immigrate (often illegally) to the United States where jobs that pay a steady income are more readily available.

When faced with markets that pay nearly nothing for conventional crops like coffee, some farmers choose to grow crops with guaranteed high-monetary yields—namely illegal drugs—like coca, from which cocaine is derived, or chat, an amphetamine-like stimulant.[10] It is, of course, dangerous to grow such crops, but it ensures that a person earns a living wage on the crops he or she grows. When the trend for coffee growers (and other types of farmers) is to lose money every year as more and more crops flood the market, the allure of actually getting paid for one's work is hard for some to ignore. This, of course, does not justify the production of illegal drugs, but it does reveal that there is always a bigger picture, a story even behind the things we don't like. And while some farmers are attempting to succeed with other high-return crops, like avocados, there remain very few legal crops that can still provide farmers with a living wage. That's why some choose to abandon farming altogether and seek work elsewhere.

LIVING WAGE: *the minimum wage necessary for a person to maintain a basic standard of living. The idea is that one's income should enable a person to provide shelter, food, heath care and education for their family.*

The search for work with a steady income leads many to choose to immigrate, both legally or illegally. Although immigration has always existed, since the passage of NAFTA in 1994, immigration to the United States has tripled (according to government numbers; relief groups say it increased tenfold).[11] The mass migration of these farmers stems from the U.S. trade policies (originally intended to help the average worker) that made their former livelihood impossible. In Guatemala, for example, coffee was once the nation's primary source of income. These days more money arrives from émigrés sending cash back from the United States.[12] These immigrants represent the human side of economic policies. To them the main issues aren't politics or increasing profit margins for multinational corporations; it is simply doing whatever they can to provide for their families.

The ongoing implications of illegal immigration continue to spark much debate in the United States, but unfortunately very little discussion occurs regarding these issues underlying illegal immigration. However, regardless of our political opinion, people like the coffee farmers who died in a 2001 border crossing in the Arizona desert[13] are our neighbors, and we are called to love them. These farmers paid a "coyote" (a smuggler) to transport them to the United States in search of better jobs. What they didn't know was that his drop-off point was sixty miles from the nearest road, in the middle of the desert—a desert that, on average, claims the life of one immigrant a day. Fourteen of these farmers (including young teenagers) died from dehydration and exposure to the elements, an incident that prompted national shock and outrage. Local churches banded together to form the group Humane Borders, which assures that the thirsty (regardless of their legal status) always have something to drink by maintaining water stations scattered around the desert.[14] This group took to heart Jesus' statement, "I was thirsty and you gave me something to drink" (Mt 25:35). Although they faced criticism for their actions, they prioritized love by deciding to serve Jesus by serving "the least of these" (Mt 25:40).

Hearing these stories challenged me into awareness about the coffee I drank. It is a strange thing to attempt to enjoy a latte when you know that it was, essentially, stolen from the people who labored to produce it for you. My four dollars didn't help the coffee farmers; it just strengthened the quarterly earnings of the corporations who took advantage of them. I don't oppose capitalism or think any other system would necessarily work better, but I find myself disturbed by economics without ethics. Any system that forces people to treat others as if their needs are less important, or as if they don't deserve proper payment for their work, seems to have strayed from the command to "love your neighbor as yourself" (Mt 19:19).

FAIR WAGES IN THE BIBLE

Scripture speaks often of how God desires his followers to treat others, and making sure workers receive the wages they deserve is strongly emphasized as one of these concerns. The book of Malachi, for instance, mentions the day of the Lord's coming, when he will be like a refiner's fire, sitting in judgment over his people and demanding acceptable offerings.

> "So I will come to put you on trial. I will be quick to testify against sorcerers, adulterers and perjurers, against those who defraud laborers of their wages, who oppress the widows and the fatherless, and deprive the foreigners among you of justice, but do not fear me," says the LORD Almighty. (Mal 3:5)

The Bible is clear that God opposes schemes to defraud laborers of their wages. These practices subvert the call to love and result in people denying the image of God in others. God called his people to standards of living that made provisions for the poor and demanded the fair payment of wages. God insisted on an economic system that cared for all of its members. In God's economy, increasing a profit margin is far less important than making sure everyone is cared for and treated rightly.

Unfortunately, it is also a common theme in Scripture for God's people to forget how they should treat others. Over and over again,

God calls the Israelites to account for their failure to care for the poor and the marginalized, and he sets up guidelines to prevent further exploitation. God's expectations aren't limited to the Israelites in the Old Testament either. James reminds Christians of how God hears the cries of the oppressed and those cheated of their wages.

> Look! The wages you failed to pay the workers who mowed your fields are crying out against you. The cries of the harvesters have reached the ears of the Lord Almighty. You have lived on earth in luxury and self-indulgence. (Jas 5:4-5)

God is aware of how our economic system harms and cheats workers, and Scripture is not silent about his indignation.

God appears most incensed when his followers participate in worship as normal while engaging in oppressive economic practices. At one point in Isaiah the people wonder why God doesn't seem to hear their prayers or respond to their humble fasts. In response, God questions how they could expect him to accept their worship when they willingly participate in the exploitation of others. God, apparently, doesn't want their worship if they are incapable of worshiping him with their entire lives—including how they treat their workers.

> "Why have we fasted," they say,
>   "and you have not seen it?
> Why have we humbled ourselves,
>   and you have not noticed?"
>
> Yet on the day of your fasting, you do as you please
>   and exploit all your workers.
> Your fasting ends in quarreling and strife,
>   and in striking each other with wicked fists.
> You cannot fast as you do today
>   and expect your voice to be heard on high.

Is this the kind of fast I have chosen,
　　only a day for people to humble themselves?
Is it only for bowing one's head like a reed
　　and for lying in sackcloth and ashes?
Is that what you call a fast,
　　a day acceptable to the LORD? (Is 58:3-5)

This passage serves as a harsh reminder that true worship doesn't merely involve enacting the cultural rituals of worship or personal piety, but more importantly, it involves how we treat others. God set up systems of fasting, personal humility and sacrifice, but those things were never to supersede or replace the commands to live justly and deal with others fairly. Following God in full obedience is an act of worship, which means that acting justly is part of what it means to worship God. As the Isaiah passage continues, it describes the sort of worship and fasting God prefers:

Is not this the kind of fasting I have chosen:
to loose the chains of injustice
　　and untie the cords of the yoke,
to set the oppressed free
　　and break every yoke?
Is it not to share your food with the hungry
　　and to provide the poor wanderer with shelter—
when you see the naked, to clothe them,
　　and not to turn away from your own flesh and blood?
(Is 58:6-7)

Worship coupled with exploitation of workers is not acceptable to God. Taking care of the needy, and treating others with love and fairness, are central attitudes and actions in the type of worship God insists on. Yet how often during our Sunday morning worship services do we even think about such things? As we clap our hands in rhythm with the latest uplifting worship song, does it ever cross our minds whether or not the coffee served out in the lobby came from farmers who received a fair wage for their work?

Those might seem like strange questions, but they haunted me as I watched the documentary about Ethiopian coffee growers, *Black Gold*. At one point the film shows a family praying that they can sell their coffee for a fair price so that their children can attend school. It seemed strange to me that our churches can participate in worship as usual while at the same time depriving these workers of their wages. If I could be the means through which God answers their prayers, by paying a fair price for my coffee, why wouldn't I do that?

Questions like these led me to seek out alternative options for how I shop. These farmers are directly affected by my consumer choices. In providing my coffee, they are, in effect, workers under my employment. Treating them with love is part of the attitude of worship God seeks. When I started shopping for alternatives, I recognized I inhabit a particular economic system that has its good and bad aspects. Opting out of the system isn't a feasible, or even desired, possibility, but I couldn't ignore the plight of the farmers—or God's words about the treatment of workers. I wanted to, as one activist put it, "never voluntarily put someone in a situation of poverty, exploitation and debt just to enjoy a cup of joe."[15] My exploration of these questions led me to discover fair trade.

TREATING WORKERS FAIRLY

Simply put, fair trade seeks to work within our current economic systems in ways that respect the dignity of the people involved and ensure that they receive fair compensation for their labor. This isn't charity, but a means of ensuring that people are treated with dignity and aren't exploited for profit. Fairly traded products receive a certification label, generally given by independent third parties that ensure certain standards for consumer goods.[16] Products that meet the fair-trade guidelines display a "Fair Trade Certified" label. These guidelines are fairly strict, but they serve to protect the worker and guarantee the consumer that fair practices were employed in producing those products.

So what do these guidelines include? First, the fair-trade label ensures that farmers receive a guaranteed minimum price for what they produce. For example, the 2008 minimum fair-trade price for coffee was set at $1.26 per pound (as compared to the average rate of $0.60-$0.70 per pound typically paid).[17] This price is a minimum, and often companies that trade fairly pay more, but at the very least, this price covers the cost of production for most farmers and is a decent living wage for many. Setting a minimum price helps ensure that the workers are not cheated of their wages.

FAIR TRADE: *a system that ensures payment of a fair price, as well as sets up fair social and environmental standards related to producing a wide variety of goods.*

However, the standards of fair trade are not just limited to fair wages. The certification also insists on fair treatment of the workers as well. Workers must be ensured safe working conditions, child labor must not be utilized, workers must be free to unionize (a necessity in countries with lax labor laws), and workers must have a democratic say in the functioning of the farming cooperative. Additionally, most organizations are set up to employ environmentally sustainable practices. The farmers often trade directly with the buyers, so as to eliminate costly (and often unscrupulous) middlemen from the process. It is a system that serves to protect the farmer and help consumers know that their money supports practices that treat people like neighbors who deserve respect—not faceless cogs in an economic machine.

When I first discovered fair trade, I appreciated having an alternative way to shop. Although the fair-trade certification for food in the United States only extends to coffee, tea and herbs, cocoa and chocolate, fresh fruit, nuts, sugar, rice, and vanilla, it is nice to know that in purchasing at least these staple items I could be assured that I wasn't supporting systems of injustice or cheating a worker of his wages. That is, I could be, *if* I could manage to find such items.

Coffee was the first item to receive fair-trade certification in 1988, but I had a hard time finding it back in 2001 when I first started to look. The large supermarket chains in my area had never heard of the term "fair trade," and even at my local Whole Foods (the nation's largest natural grocery food chain) an employee told me that they didn't see the need to carry stuff like that. Starbucks claimed to carry a fair-trade coffee, but it was never in stock in any of the stores in my area. Eventually I started purchasing my coffee at Ten Thousand Villages—a gift store run by the Mennonites that sells fairly traded handicrafts and consumer goods from around the world.[18] I discovered that the coffee did cost more than the vacuum-sealed cans I had previously been purchasing at the gro-cery store, but it cost less than other specialty coffees and tasted far superior. Since then, as awareness of fair trade has grown, I can regularly find fairly traded coffee and tea at my local grocery store and at big-box chains like Target. Other items like sugar, vanilla and spices are now in some supermarkets, as well as at specialty stores like Whole Foods and Trader Joe's. But even if you don't live near stores that carry fair-trade items, you can find them online at places like Equalexchange.com or even Amazon.com.

Fair trade certification isn't a perfect system. It doesn't claim to solve all the injustices in our economic system today, and like any system, it can be abused. As the public becomes aware of the avail-ability of fairly traded goods, more and more corporations jump on the bandwagon, trying to capitalize on the idea. You can even find fair-trade lines put out by the major coffee companies like Nestlé. Some people balk at the idea of giving any more money to the companies that caused so much of the problem in the first place, but others see it as an opportunity to send a message to those companies that consumers support fair labor practices. Fair trade is simply one way to work within our given economic system to care for others, and whatever its problems, it makes huge differences in individual lives.

For example, as the Rwandan village of Kizi struggled to rebuild from the 1994 genocide that ravaged the country, a fair-trade coffee co-op helped the town survive. This co-op currently employs over a thousand farmers and helped them earn 30 percent more for their labors than they did growing conventional coffee.[19] The establishment of the coffee co-op helped transform the village from one of the poorest in the world to a community with a functioning and hopeful economy. Besides giving the farmers fair wages, the co-op has also contributed to the town by building a school and providing shoes for the children. As one farmer commented, "It has helped with everything, the money for school fees, the kids. I'm 100 per cent for it. . . . The co-op is . . . like a mother with enough milk to feed all her children."[20]

These are people helped by fair trade. Many of the farmers were children during the genocide and witnessed their countrymen treating each other as worthless objects to be destroyed. Then they faced a global economy that treated producers as worthless pawns in the game of increasing corporate profit. But finally they found a system that would treat them as people and help them rebuild their lives.

Even if fair trade doesn't solve every problem, it is still effective in improving the lives of workers, and it is a worthwhile endeavor. Of course, many farmers still struggle under unfair labor conditions and don't receive a fair wage for their work. If we are to take seriously the command to love our neighbor, we need to find ways to treat these workers with love, and that includes refraining from participating in unfair practices. Similarly, if we as Christians seek to engage in worship that God deems acceptable, then we (as

individuals and as churches) must cease exploiting workers—
whether directly or complicitly. Fair trade offers us one way to do
just that.

Supporting fair trade. Here are a few ways that you can support
fair trade.

1. Buy fair trade. Okay, I know it's the obvious suggestion, but it
needs to be said. By purchasing fairly traded items, we not only
ensure the producers were paid fair wages for their work but we
also send a message to corporate entities that we care about how
people are treated. We are, in a sense, voting with our money for
the fair and ethical treatment of workers. Yes, it will most likely
require some sacrifices from average consumers as they adjust
their budgets to buy slightly more expensive products—which are
generally more expensive because workers actually get paid for
their work! As is often the case, our savings usually come out of
someone else's pocket. However, the extra expense is worth it to
subvert exploitation. Next time you buy coffee (or tea, sugar,
spices, vanilla, rice, fruit or nuts) look for the fair-trade label and
choose to consume ethically.

2. Ask your local stores to carry fairly traded items. Most companies are eager to meet the demands of their customers, so tell
them of your interest in purchasing fairly traded items. If you
don't ask they will never know that there is local demand. Get
your friends to ask as well: more voices mean greater demand.
And of course, if they start carrying the items you asked for, be
sure to buy them there.

*3. Get your church to serve fairly traded coffee and tea during the
fellowship time.* If worship acceptable to God means that his people
are not exploiting workers, it just makes sense to care about what
kind of labor practices the church supports with the coffee it
serves. Check out Equal Exchange's Interfaith Program (http://
interfaith.equalexchange.com) that helps churches extend their
fellowship to coffee farmers by providing churches with educa-

tional resources, information regarding how to promote fair trade and opportunities to purchase fairly traded goods in bulk.

4. *Raise awareness.* Talk about fair trade with your friends and family. Write about it for your local newspaper or church newsletter. Post information on your website or blog. Write to the major coffee companies and tell them that you support fair-trade practices. Write to your government representatives and let them know that their constituents care about how trade policies affect the lives of real people. The more you talk about it, the more people you can help get onboard to support alternative economic practices that value loving people more than loving money.

Fair-trade labeling. In one way, buying fair trade is easy, especially when the items are labeled. However, many other ventures out there practice fair trade but, for one reason or another, are not fair-trade certified. Finding these options will require being a conscientious consumer who takes the time to discover the story behind what you are buying—even if you have to read more online. Many companies that care enough to put the money and effort into an ethically produced product will want you to know about it, so get into reading labels and researching more about the products you like.

I recently heard Christian author Brian McLaren speak on justice issues at a local bookstore. At one point he suggested labeling products with "ethical facts," similar to the "nutrition facts" already found on food products. The nutrition label is required so that consumers know (for the most part) what the food they are about to eat contains. A similar kind of ethics label would serve to inform the consumer regarding the history behind what they are buying. Were the workers paid fair wages? Are they being treated humanely in the workplace? Were hazardous pesticides and other chemicals used on this product? Was it grown in sustainable ways? Those desiring to make informed and ethical choices as they shop would then have more resources to help them make decisions.

Of course, just as there are many people who ignore the litany of unhealthy and unnatural products listed on food labels, there would still be consumers who couldn't care less about the people who produced the product they are consuming. Even still, this could be a useful step in helping raise awareness. We as consumers have the right to ask companies (and the government) to provide such labeling, to let them know that we want to know those facts. If corporations and governments have nothing to hide or be ashamed of, then such labeling would do nothing but boost their sales.

Fair-trade businesses. The more adventurous and entrepreneurial out there could even start their own businesses that work with farming collectives to help guarantee them a fair price and market for their labors. For example, a ministry group in Douglas, Arizona, was concerned by the political rhetoric regarding immigration. So, with a deep care for their friends across the border, this group decided to help thirty Mexican families achieve their dream: staying in Mexico and farming their own land. A $20,000 loan, secured from a Presbyterian group, helped a handful of Mexican farmers set up Café Justo, "a cooperative venture to harvest, roast, package and deliver their own crop to America's booming java market."[21] These farmers take ownership of the entire process from growing the beans to delivering the product to the consumer, and they earn fair prices for their work. It took the commitment of a few caring people who weren't comfortable witnessing economic injustice and who weren't satisfied with status quo solutions to realize that they could be the ones to make a difference. For this group, seeking everyday justice became their pursuit, and they made the lives of others better along the way.[22]

Others, like eight-year-old Lauren in North Carolina, use what resources they have at the moment to help coffee farmers. The Land of a Thousand Hills[23] fair-trade coffee company involves churches in healing and developing Rwanda through fair-trade coffee endeavors, encouraging Christians to "Drink coffee. Do good." Inspired by their ministry, in November of 2008, Lauren baked 1,250 cookies to sell under the tag line "Eat cookies. Do good." With the help of her parents, Lauren advertised her bake sale all over town and ended up making $3,600 from her culinary efforts. She then used this money to buy fourteen cargo bikes for coffee farmers in Rwanda to use to safely transport their coffee beans. Everyday things like bicycles and bake sales can make huge differences in individual lives.[24]

CONCLUSION

Becoming an ethical consumer may take creative steps like seeking new labeling systems or starting new businesses, or it could be as simple as tweaking your shopping habits. If we are to attempt to live justly in the everyday, how we shop is one of the most basic habits that we can alter. Where we choose to spend our money affects not just us or the large corporations but everyday people around the globe. If we care for these people and love them as Jesus commanded us to, we need to be aware of the ways our economic choices affect them. Making sure they receive fair wages through programs like fair trade is one way to put love into action.

FOR MORE INFORMATION

Books

Alvarez, Julia. *A Cafecito Story.* White River Junction, Vt.: Chelsea Green Publishing, 2004. This story is about a man who leaves the Midwest to explore the roots of coffee and ends up spending his life developing a fair-trade enterprise.

Cycon, Dean. *Javatrekker: Dispatches from the World of Fair Trade Coffee.* White River Junction, Vt.: Chelsea Green Publishing,

2007. An introduction to the people who make our coffee; considers the global issues affecting their lives.

Stiglitz, Joseph E., and Andrew Charlton. *Fair Trade for All: How Trade Can Promote Development.* Oxford: Oxford University Press, 2007. By an economist who won the Nobel Prize, this book offers an in-depth look at global trade practices and fair-trade options.

Wild, Anthony. *Coffee: A Dark History.* New York: W. W. Norton, 2004. This is a history of coffee that explores its connection with exploitation through the centuries.

Movies

Black Gold. Codirected and coproduced by Nick and Marc Francis. 78 min., Fulcrum Productions, 2006. A documentary on Ethiopian coffee farmers seeking a fair price for their efforts.

Buyer Be Fair. Written and directed by John de Graaf. 57 min., Fox-Wilmar Productions, 2006. A documentary overview of fair-trade certification, and how it helps people and the environment.

Websites

TransFairUSA
www.transfairusa.org
The organization behind the fair-trade certification in the United States

Equal Exchange
www.equalexchange.com
Fair-trade organization that provides resources, runs co-operatives and sells fairly traded goods

Fair Trade Federation
www.fairtradefederation.org
An association of businesses committed to fair trade

Make Trade Fair
www.maketradefair.com
Oxfam International's advocacy site for fair-trade issues

Interfaith Working Group on Trade and Investment
www.tradejusticeusa.org
Organization of faith groups involved in public discussions on trade issues

2

Chocolate

MODERN-DAY SLAVERY EXPOSED

Gavin raced into his house behind his sister, his Superman cape fluttering behind him. Cheeks flushed from the cool autumn air, he immediately dumped this year's trick-or-treat bounty onto the living room floor. Gavin loved Halloween. He'd decided on his costume back in July and had literally counted the days up to this candy jackpot. Now with a wealth of candy arrayed before him, he and his sister commenced with the serious task of trading their favorites.

"Now remember, you only get to eat two pieces tonight. We'll save the rest for later," his mom called in from the other room.

"Well, whatever's left after I get a chance to raid the stash," his dad added with a laugh, causing the kids to let out an exasperated, "Dad!!!"

Just then Gavin held up a small bag of gold-coin candy. "Oh cool," he exclaimed, "pirate gold." He ripped the bag open and took out one of the coins. Stamped on the gold foil were the words "Slave Free. Fairly Traded."

"Dad," Gavin asked, "what does that mean? I thought Abraham

Lincoln got rid of slavery—at least that's what my teacher said."

"He did," his father replied as he picked up the bag Gavin had thrown aside. Attached to the bag was a small note that read "Chocolate is a treat, but it is a trick for many children who are forced into slavery to produce it. Help make chocolate a treat for everyone by supporting slave-free, fair-trade candy."

Gavin looked at his dad with shock. "You mean there are kids in slavery today who are forced to make chocolate? That's just wrong."

Hearing this exchange, his mom walked into the room and gave his dad a withering look. "Sweetie," she said to Gavin, "I'm not sure what this card is talking about, but it isn't something that you need to worry about. Let's pick up the rest of this candy and get you guys off to bed. It's late, and Halloween or not, you still have school tomorrow."

Gavin reluctantly obeyed, but as he cleared the last of the candy away, he considered his Superman costume. His mom had said that children being in slavery wasn't something he should worry about, but he thought that a real superhero would do exactly what Abraham Lincoln had done and put an end to slavery.

☛

In March 2004, Tony van de Keuken of the Netherlands walked into a public prosecutor's office and asked to be arrested.[1] His crime? Eating chocolate.

Tony understood the sobering reality that thousands of children are forced to work in the cocoa farms of Côte d'Ivoire—where most of the world's cocoa (the beans from which we make chocolate) grows. He realized that child slavery taints most of the chocolate produced in the world. In the Netherlands, it is illegal, and punishable by up to four years in prison, to purchase something you know was obtained using criminal methods. So Tony ate some chocolate and asked the prosecutors to arrest him as a chocolate criminal. The way he saw it, as a consumer of chocolate, he knowingly supported the systems of child labor and human slavery. Tony's case made international news and eventually made it to the Dutch Supreme Court, which even heard the testimonies of former child slaves.[2] The judge ended up dismissing the case on the grounds that prosecutors have the right to decide not to press charges.[3]

THE PROBLEM WITH CHOCOLATE

I'm not really a sweets person, but I love a good piece of dark chocolate. It's hard to imagine there being any problem with something so delectable. Exchanged as a token of love on Valentine's Day, hidden in brightly colored eggs at Easter time, and dropped into the awaiting buckets of princesses and pirates at Halloween, chocolate represents more than just a tasty indulgence; it is a cultural symbol. It is also a megaindustry. In 2000, people in the United States consumed 3.3 billion pounds of chocolate, spending nearly $13 billion to supply that habit.[4] Yet the media's repeated reports on the appalling conditions in cocoa farms has cast a shadow over this sweet treat.

The majority of the world's cocoa beans grow in West Africa—especially in the countries of Cameroon, Nigeria, Ghana and Côte d'Ivoire, nations struggling to overcome poverty and unrest. Farmers sell these beans to the world's major chocolate producers, like Hershey's, Nestlé and Mars. So the beans from these countries are the source of most of the chocolate those of us in Western countries consume.

But where our chocolate comes from rarely crosses the mind of the average consumer. We are most interested in simply enjoying it for its taste—or finding it on sale. If we ask if certain chocolate products are good, we mean "Are they yummy?" We don't mean "Were they ethically produced?" Indeed, for many of us (unless we are referring to Willy Wonka's Oompa-Loompas), workers in chocolate factories and cocoa farms are rarely the subject of our attention. It's a different story in cocoa-producing countries. In Côte d'Ivoire, the government estimates that around half of the country's 14 million inhabitants participate directly or indirectly in the production of cocoa.[5] For them chocolate is, literally, life.

Yet media reports reveal the often horrific working conditions in the cocoa farms. These reports indicate that there are high numbers of children working to harvest cocoa beans. While children generally lend a hand on the family farm in agriculturally based societies, these children typically aren't family, or even local, but instead have been trafficked in from neighboring countries. These children face starvation and beatings, and many are forced to work for little or no pay.

HUMAN TRAFFICKING: the illegal and generally involuntary smuggling of a person across borders, often for the purposes of forced labor.

These revelations have caused an international stir, and when the information first came out, investigations commenced immediately by many government and nongovernment organizations. The reports they produced were shocking. In 2000, the U.S. State Department revealed that, although child labor, human trafficking and forced labor are all prohibited in Côte d'Ivoire, all three are still commonly practiced.[6] Another report produced two years later by the International Institute of Tropical Agriculture revealed that an "estimated 284,000 children are working on cocoa farms in hazardous tasks such as using machetes and applying pesticides and insecticides without the necessary protective equipment."[7] The report also indicated strong evidence of human trafficking. Such practices are illegal worldwide, and the United States even forbids the import of goods made from forced child labor.[8]

Yet these practices are often overlooked or ignored by the companies that the farms supply. The result? Much of the chocolate we consume has its roots in child labor, often forced or slave labor. Like Tony van de Keuken, most of us are guilty of aiding criminal behavior, even slavery, every time we indulge in a chocolaty treat.

I don't doubt that nearly all of us morally oppose forcing children into slavery. We may feel tricked into unknowingly participating in oppression just because we like to eat chocolate, but the problems *continue* because most people, like Gavin's family above, are unaware that they exist at all. We are, in a sense, victims of a system that causes us to be victimizers. No parent would request the kidnapping, beating and starving of other children so that they could serve chocolate cupcakes at their child's birthday party, but nonetheless, this is essentially what happens.

These children, most of whom have never even had the chance to taste chocolate, are caught in broken systems that are ready to take advantage of their vulnerability. Problems exist at all levels—from production companies, to local governments and local militias, to the farmers themselves. It is hard to point a finger and identify just one source of the problems. Unfortunately, that also means that easy solutions aren't readily available, prompting the need for multifaceted and creative approaches.

To better understand the problem, we need to look at the plight of the cocoa farmer. As with coffee, the market price for cocoa beans steadily dropped during the years surrounding the turn of the most recent millennium. At the same time, unstable governments and military groups continued to impose multiple (and often illegal) taxes on the farmers for growing, transporting and selling their goods. Farmers, desperate to turn a profit, started looking for the cheapest labor they could find. Tragically, that need for cheap labor has sometimes resulted in children trafficked into slavery.

Aly Diabate was such a boy tricked into slavery. To an eleven-year-old boy living in the impoverished West African country of Mali, the chance to help support his family by working on a cocoa farm was too good to ignore. The offer of $150 a year and a bicycle sealed the deal for Aly, and he took the job, which was supposedly local. But instead, the slave trader trafficked Aly to Côte d'Ivoire where his only rewards were beatings with bicycle chains. Aly reported having to work whenever the sun was up and being locked into crowded, poorly ventilated rooms at night. He often had nightmares about dying in the cocoa fields.

Aly's ordeal ended when a fellow slave escaped and brought the police to witness the conditions on the farm. The boy returned home to Mali while the slaver served only twenty-four days in jail.[9] Yet Aly was just one of an estimated 15,000 children in agricultural slavery in Côte d'Ivoire. His nightmares remain a reality for others picking the cocoa beans for our chocolate, others who similarly cry out for release from this oppression. His story should remind us of the affirmation in the Psalms that,

> You, LORD, hear the desire of the afflicted;
>> you encourage them, and you listen to their cry,
> defending the fatherless and the oppressed,
>> so that mere earthly mortals
>> will never again strike terror. (Ps 10:17-18)

Growing numbers of children like Aly face oppression and experience the terror of slavery—all for the sake of chocolate. As their enslavement continues, it often seems like their cries aren't heard by anyone. Like Gavin's parents, too many believe that slavery is a thing of the past, something dealt with once and for all over a century ago. It is hard to effect change, or make a difference for these children, when most of the world is unaware that the problem even exists.

MODERN-DAY SLAVERY

Researchers estimate that there are more slaves in the world today than there were during the four hundred years of the African slave trade during the colonial era. The current estimate stands at 27 million.[10] But unlike the African slave trade, where slavers sold humans openly on the streets, the slave trade today operates mostly underground.

Lies and false papers help traffic children and women (and occasionally men) across borders into slavery. Often these slaves find themselves in strange lands forced to work as laborers or prostitutes. Around the world (including in the United States) slaves work publicly in restaurants, factories, laundry facilities, cleaning services and in the sex trade, but they remain silent out of fear. They have no language skills to seek aid with, and they fear punishment as illegal immigrants or prostitutes if they try to escape.[11] They are often threatened with beatings or actually beaten for not working hard enough, or they are drugged into being "more willing" sex-trade victims.

An estimated 27 million people are in slavery in the world today.

The children who are forced into slavery at very young ages are often brainwashed into believing that a life of slavery is the only possible way of life. The 2008 documentary *Call+Response* opens with the heart-wrenching scene of just such a group of children: six-year-old girls forced to work in a brothel, knowing no other life besides offering sex to men. Such children are common worldwide as greed, debt and perversion lead some to choose vices above the dignity and value of a human being.

These slaves exist because it is profitable to others for them to exist. There is a market for cheap labor, for cheap chocolate, for cheap sex. Choosing to value these slaves as people (as children, for goodness' sake!) more than we value the economic benefits they provide is part of what it will take to abolish modern-day slavery. It may seem like a daunting task, but at least in the Christian tradition, there is a long history of taking a stand against slavery.

SLAVERY IN THE BIBLE

In ancient Near Eastern cultures, slavery existed publicly as a normal part of life. People owned, used and often abused slaves. The standard line of thought held that slaves were property to be used as one desired. Slaves weren't treated as neighbors to be loved or fellow image-bearers deserving respect; in fact the entire system undermined the command to love God and love others. In light of such disrespect for God's creation and his commands, you might expect the institution of slavery to be outright condemned in the Bible. Instead, the issue of slavery in the Bible is complicated. What we find are passages dictating how slaves and masters should treat each other, examples of biblical "heroes" owning slaves, and even laws that were put in place to protect slaves—yet no condemnation of slavery itself.

This lack of condemnation is a cause of concern for many. What we know about God and the way of life that Christ calls us to makes it difficult to reconcile living that life if it includes the dehumanizing institution of slavery. But it doesn't help that, until the nineteenth century, it was common for the majority of Christians to read the Bible as not only approving of but mandating slavery as a God-ordained institution. The proponents of slavery interpreted the existence of slavery in the Bible to imply that God created some people inferior, intending for them to be slaves. That idea, when mixed with racist assumptions, led to horrific actions like the forced enslavement of Africans—under the guise of biblical justification. While a thorough discussion of slavery in the Bible is outside the scope of this book, I want to offer an alternative way of reading the biblical response to slavery.

As I mentioned earlier, slavery existed as an accepted institution in biblical times. Under the Romans, slavery formed the very backbone of the economy. In Roman Italy, an estimated one third of the population were slaves.[12] The Jews, an oppressed people under Roman occupation, were in some ways just one step away from slavery themselves, and to challenge the military oppressors and the stability of the economy would most likely have resulted in quick imprisonment or execution. Jesus challenging the supremacy of the Roman Empire was likely one of the primary, human motivators for his execution at the hands of the Roman authorities. So for Jesus' followers to pen abolitionist mantras would have been a dangerous act of subversion, resulting in a swift end to the Jesus movement. The biblical writers had to take care in how they expressed the gospel's challenge to the injustices of their society. Thus we find no outright condemnations of slavery in Scripture. The biblical writers were more interested in undermining the very roots of injustice by replacing the mindset that made slavery possible with a mindset of love for God and neighbor, which left no room for such oppression. This revolution of love was, of course, gradual as it worked its way into the hearts of Christ's followers.

So while Scripture doesn't overtly condemn slavery, neither is the status quo upheld. What we find instead are subtle challenges intended to subvert imperial oppression, including the institution of slavery.[13] In many Roman households, indeed, slaves were treated as nothing more than property. A master could beat, starve or even rape a slave since it was his right to treat his property however he desired. In light of such a system, hear the revolutionary undertones of Paul's statements in Ephesians and Colossians: "And masters, treat your slaves in the same way [that slaves are to obey and serve their masters]. Do not threaten them, since you know that he who is both their Master and yours is in heaven, and there is no favoritism with him" (Eph 6:9), and, "Masters, provide your slaves with what is right and fair, because you know that you also have a Master in heaven" (Col 4:1). These statements undermine the belief that slaves are mere property, and instead suggest that both slaves and human masters are equally servants of God, which introduces the idea that all people deserve to be treated rightly. This comes across most strongly in Paul's letter to Philemon, which he wrote on behalf of Philemon's escaped slave Onesimus. Paul publicly implores fellow believers to see this man not as a slave, but as a brother and partner in Christ. While not threatening the very survival of the early Jesus movement by overtly demanding the complete abolition of slavery, these kinds of statements erase the social distinctions between slaves and masters, calling for the practice of a new social order within the Christian community.

The Christians in Paul's day had little power to directly challenge the Roman Empire's economic or political systems, but within their own alternative communities, they could encourage each other to love and treat slaves as equals worthy of respect. For many this involved opting out of the system entirely: granting those in bondage freedom in the name of Christ. Slavery wasn't condoned; it was challenged and subverted in the name of love. In the spirit of this love, nineteenth-century abolitionists used the freedom of their democratic societies to call for an end to slavery in their time.

SEEKING ABOLITION THEN

The nineteenth-century hymn "O Holy Night" is one of my favorite Christmas carols, but for years I sang it (off-key and with gusto) without really considering the lyrics. I thought it was just a pretty song about the night Jesus was born. Yet shortly after the release of the original French version in 1847, a French bishop denounced the song for its "lack of musical taste and total absence of the spirit of religion."[14] Apparently its author, Placide Cappeau, faced opposition for his extreme political views, namely his opposition to inequality, slavery, injustice and other kinds of oppression. The bishop didn't consider such stances to represent proper religious values. Fortunately for us, the minister who (loosely) translated the song into English shared Cappeau's values as well. The themes of justice and opposition to slavery appear in the lines

> Truly He taught us to love one another;
> His law is love and His gospel is peace.
> Chains shall He break, for the slave is our brother;
> And in His name all oppression shall cease.[15]

This song captures Paul's message to Philemon, a message seemingly forgotten in most of the church by the nineteenth century. Yet a few brave people were willing to adopt unpopular, "extreme" views because they recognized those views in the Bible. They grasped the revolutionary nature of the call to embrace the slave as our brother, and thus they took on the challenge of ending slavery in their own day. This wasn't just a social movement; this was a spiritual commitment to seek justice and love their neighbor. And despite opposition, they succeeded.

The 2007 movie *Amazing Grace* brought renewed attention to the story of one of these abolitionists, William Wilberforce (1759-1833). Born into a world where the enslavement of Africans was a common practice, Wilberforce devoted much of his life to ending the slave trade, improving working conditions for slaves and, finally, abolishing slavery in British territories altogether. The world in which he lived was much like our world today—a world that enjoyed the "benefits" of slavery but had little understanding of the practice itself. Consumers cherished the wealth, as well as the luxury goods like sugar and molasses, that slavery brought to England. People appreciated the prosperity these things signified, but they often didn't know their true cost in human lives. To many, slavery was an idea, part of an economic system that represented the way the world worked. To challenge such an institution was to challenge history and reject prosperity. It took coming to see the slave as a brother or sister to soften their hearts.

For Wilberforce, his abolitionist work began with a dramatic conversion to evangelical Christianity. After struggling with religion in his younger years, he finally saw that "religion was not what happened when one picked up a Bible or entered church, but was about living every moment of life in the presence and to the glory of God."[16] This religious commitment took hold of him and informed his perspective on social issues like slavery. He came to the realization that his money and his time were not his own. As one writer describes, Wilberforce saw that "it all belonged to God and had been given to him to use for God's purposes and according to God's will. God had blessed him so he, in turn, might bless others, especially those less fortunate than himself."[17] As a result, he gave away much of his money and devoted his time to justice issues, like the abolition of slavery and animal welfare. He surrounded himself with like-minded friends who encouraged him to take the biblical command to love one's neighbor literally, whether that neighbor was British or African. To them slavery wasn't just part of a historic economic system; it represented a failure to love their neighbor. So they set about to effect change on a massive scale.

First, they had to help the public understand the realities of slavery, and move them toward compassion and love for the slaves. The general public saw slavery as a fact of life, an unavoidable part of the economic system. Defenders of slavery argued that abolishing it would weaken the economy, take jobs away from British citizens, strengthen their enemies and actually harm Africans who were "benefiting" from slavery.[18] It was not uncommon for slaves to be seen as subhuman, often being compared to animals. Through a nationwide campaign, abolitionists worked to challenge all these assumptions and to "inform and inflame" the public regarding slavery.[19] They circulated illustrations of the conditions of slave ships, which horrified the average British citizen who had no idea that such atrocities occurred. Activists sent letters to magazines and newspapers, describing these conditions and imploring for an end to such practices. From the pulpit, pastors told the stories of slavery and its dehumanizing conditions. Artists created brooches and posters, and popular songwriters wrote songs to spread the message. Boycotts on goods obtained by slave labor (like sugar) commenced, and at one point, an estimated 300,000 people (rich and poor people and businesses alike) gave up using sugar tainted by the forced employ of slaves.[20] Slowly this campaign of information and awareness affected the social consciousness of the nation. In 1807, Wilberforce finally saw Parliament ban the British slave trade, and in 1833, just two days before he died, he saw the passage of an act to abolish slavery altogether.[21]

The antislavery movement, which Wilberforce's Christian convictions pushed him to fight for, had significant implications around the world. Although it took another thirty years and a bloody civil war to abolish slavery in the United States, he helped shift the basic worldview pertaining to slavery. In choosing to love the slave as his neighbor, as the Bible commands, Wilberforce challenged the assumption that slavery was an unavoidable reality. Author Eric Metaxas comments, "The idea that [slavery] is inextricably intertwined with human civilization, and part of the way things are supposed to be, and economically necessary and morally defensible, is gone."[22] This shift in perspective is what helped end the African slave trade in the nineteenth century, and although slavery still exists in the world today, it is illegal and never seen as morally defensible. Today, it is the end of illegal slavery that modern abolitionists seek.

SEEKING ABOLITION TODAY

Encourage elected officials to support laws that seek justice. Even though slavery is generally rejected—considered morally reprehensible in our modern world—it still flourishes. Those who keep slaves see the economic benefit they provide as more important than their worth as human beings. Others prioritize their own needs by using people as objects—be that as forced sex slaves, forced maids or forced laborers. But most people are simply ignorant of the widespread issue of slavery in today's world. Because it is hidden, it is difficult to know that the chocolate we eat may have come from child slave labor—or that the women doing our laundry were forced into that job. As it was in Wilberforce's day, we need an information campaign to help spread the word. I appreciate David Batstone's book *Not for Sale* and his audacity in telling story after story of modern-day slavery (many of these stories took place in the United States). Likewise, the 2008 documentary *Call+Response* brought together musicians, activists and politicians to inform people about slavery and human trafficking. Injustice flourishes in the dark; bringing these stories into the light can be the first step in abolishing slavery today.

Despite the vastness of the problem, modern-day abolitionists do exist and are working hard to end worldwide slavery. Ending the slave connection to chocolate is a major part of that endeavor. For instance, as reports appeared that exposed child slave labor in the cocoa industry, and even as the major chocolate companies admitted that problems existed, consumers and legislatures saw the need for slave-free chocolate. Since importing products made by slave labor is technically illegal in the United States, some concerned lawmakers and consumers began to look for ways to guarantee that companies were truly importing only slave-free products.

In 2001, U.S. Representative Eliot Engel introduced an amendment to the *2002 Agriculture Appropriations Bill* to set aside $250,000 for the Food and Drug Administration to develop "slave free" labeling requirements on cocoa products.[23] The House of Representatives approved the bill by a vote of 291-115 in June 2001. Unfortunately many of the major chocolate companies wouldn't legally qualify for a "no slave labor" label to be put on their product and weren't happy about legislation insisting they had to. The big chocolate companies hired former U.S. presidential candidate Bob Dole to lobby their cause to the Senate.[24] He helped them reach a "compromise" that avoided mandatory legislation but had them agree to the "Harkin-Engel Protocol," which said they would voluntarily put an end to forced child labor on cocoa farms by July 2005. That deadline passed with no change, and the companies then received an extension until July 2008 to comply.

Despite such efforts, governmental and journalistic studies published in early 2008 found no measurable change in the conditions on the cocoa farms or in the social infrastructure that might help prevent such slavery. When asked why this was the case, William Guyton, president of the World Cocoa Foundation, replied, "the Harkin-Engel protocol is something that has never been attempted before in any agricultural sector or any sector to speak of."[25] Guyton suggested that ending slavery and changing an economy had never been done before, so they really didn't know where to begin!

Those who know the history of abolitionists like William Wilberforce, or even the reform movements to end child labor in the United States a century ago, would beg to differ with his excuse. Difficult though it was, the advocates who fought to end slavery and protect children succeeded in their cause. But it took the combined willingness and effort of the government, social organizations, businesses and concerned citizens to effect this change. Ending modern-day slavery and reforming the production of chocolate will require similar resolve and effort, but neither are impossible goals.

Even as the Harkin-Engel Protocol faces scrutiny and revision, other laws are in the works that seek to abolish slavery today. In December 2007, the U.S. House of Representatives passed the *William Wilberforce Trafficking Victims Protection Reauthorization Act*

(H.R. 3887).[26] This act, named after the famous abolitionist, extended funding to combat human trafficking. Encouraging our elected officials to support such laws is an everyday way to seek justice for those oppressed in slavery.

Use your purchasing power as a consumer. One of the simplest ways to effect change is to use your power as a consumer. Candy companies rely on impulse buys for 90 percent of their sales.[27] Altering this everyday action can send a huge message to the chocolate companies. If you choose to buy fairly traded or "slave-free" chocolate, you are telling those companies that you care about issues like slavery and that you refuse to be complicit in supporting such practices. I know it's hard to say no to the Snickers seduction in the checkout lane at the grocery store, but the candy companies are counting on that. So even though it might take a little more self-discipline, seeking out slave-free options helps create an alternative economy that tries to avoid hurting others for profit.

Slave-free chocolate for snacking, drinking or baking is not really that hard to find either. In many stores it simply means leaving the impulse-buy aisle for the specialty candy section. Slave-free options are also widely available online. Companies like Serrv (www.serrv.org), Global Exchange (www.globalexchange.org) and even Amazon (www.amazon.com) all offer slave-free chocolate—often including even seasonal items like Halloween and Easter candies. Purchasing your chocolate from these sources impacts the market and shows that there is a demand for products produced without slave labor. However, to end the horror for children right now, more active steps are necessary.

Write to the chocolate companies. As a consumer, you can also send direct messages to the major chocolate companies like Nestlé and Mars to let them know that you care about how they produce their chocolate. Write letters or e-mails, asking them to abide by the Harkin-Engel Protocol like they promised. Ask them to move

beyond vague statements of concern for these issues and find ways
to guarantee that the chocolate you buy is slave-free. Let them
know that you don't appreciate that the cost of cheap chocolate is
ultimately paid by children and that you are willing to pay a fair
price for ethically produced items. These companies exist to make
money and do so by meeting the demands of their customers.
Voicing your concerns is an everyday action you can do to help fix
this broken system.

Raise awareness. Others can take this a step further by working to raise awareness about these issues and get others onboard
with the campaign to end slavery. A great example of this occurred in early 2007 when three children from South London
took a stand for slave-free chocolate. These kids, upset by discovering that enslaved children made the chocolate they ate,
chose to insist on a slave-free Easter, and they staged their plea
in front of a Nestlé factory. Holding Easter eggs with signs that
said, "Warning—this product may contain the blood, sweat and
tears of African child slaves," these kids called for an end to selling slave-made chocolate. Nine-year-old participant Jermaine
Nelson commented, "We wrote a letter to Tony Blair to tell him
how we feel about slavery, because if we don't tell him he won't
do anything about it. We drew around our hands and sent the
pictures to show him that children are small and shouldn't be
working so hard."[28]

These kids used their voices to give a voice to children in slavery. It took courage and self-sacrifice for these kids to write the
prime minister and go to the Nestlé factory, but their effort represents a commitment to care for the needs of others. By looking
beyond themselves and discovering what they could do where
they were at, they helped other children suffering from oppression. At the time, the major British chocolate companies responded
that it would be nearly impossible to guarantee slave-free chocolate. But just two years later, in March 2009, Cadbury announced

that their milk chocolate bars (England's top-selling chocolate bar) would be fair-trade, slave-free certified by the summer of 2009.[29] This huge step forward in the campaign to end modern-day slavery demonstrates the power of consumers raising their voices for justice.

EVERYDAY PRACTITIONER

Alexa Shaich, student
Seattle, Washington

Alexa was a typical high-school student. But during her senior year, she became a modern-day abolitionist as well.

During a student government class, a friend brought up the issue of modern-day slavery. Having learned about it in her church youth group, Alexa's friend wanted to spread this knowledge to her classmates. Alexa was shocked to discover the extent of modern-day slavery and that her hometown of Seattle was a major port for human trafficking. She thought about what it would be like if she or one of her friends were forced into slavery, and she knew she had to take action.

With her classmates, Alexa helped organize an information campaign. They invited twenty other local schools to attend events that helped raised awareness about modern-day slavery. But Alexa decided to do even more. For her senior project she organized a benefit dinner to help fight slavery. The purpose of the dinner was twofold: to educate people about modern-day slavery and to raise funds for the International Justice Mission (IJM), which works to free slaves worldwide.

Alexa poured herself into this event, recruiting her friends and family to help out. Her mother's restaurant catered the event, and her brother created a registration and information website (www.endhumanslavery.com). She invited speakers from IJM and the Seattle police department to talk about the magnitude of slavery.

The dinner proved to be a great success, as Alexa raised nearly $5,000 to help end slavery. She also raised awareness in her community and had numerous people tell her that they had no idea slavery was still such a major issue. Alexa worked within her everyday world to seek justice for those in slavery. Even as a high-school student she knew that she could make a difference. Reflecting on her experience, Alexa expressed her hope "that by raising awareness about human trafficking people will realize that this isn't just a big issue in other countries, it's happening right here! And I hope that they know that there are so many things all of us can be doing, big or small, to make a difference."[30]

Financially support or volunteer with organizations that seek justice for slaves and make slavery unnecessary. Other organizations exist where you can get directly involved in freeing those trapped in slavery around the world. International Justice Mission (IJM), for instance, sends in legal representatives to investigate and rescue the victims of slavery.[31] Most countries do not legally allow slavery, but nevertheless, they often do nothing to combat it. IJM seeks to uphold those laws and restore hope to those needing justice. They not only help free those trapped in slavery (often as sex slaves), but they also provide aftercare services to help the victims establish a new life. They seek justice in a way that restores and heals. In addition to financial support, these sorts of organizations need volunteers (especially those with a background in law) to help investigate problems worldwide and to ensure that proper steps are taken to see that true justice happens.

Organizations like IJM not only rescue individuals, they also help

create an environment where slavery cannot flourish. When governments and local law enforcement agencies are pressured to actually
uphold antislavery laws, the presence of slavery dwindles. But laws
are often not enough. Slavery thrives in areas where people have no
safety net—no education, no government assistance, no recourse to
loans to start businesses. Finding ways to provide these services re-
duces the likelihood of desperate people being tricked into slavery.
Supporting education and job-training programs and providing
small businesses microloans (through groups like Kiva[32]) are all
steps we can take to eliminate
the economic climate that pro-
motes slavery in the first place.

Providing the safety nets of education, job-training and microloans for small businesses can help eliminate the conditions that allow slavery to thrive.

CONCLUSION

And remember Tony, the guy
who tried to get himself arrested for eating chocolate? He
knew that something had to be
done to address the problem so
that people would no longer
have to choose between eating chocolate and oppressing others.
He started producing his own slave-free chocolate bars. His chocolate comes from a farming collective in Ghana that insists on fair
labor practices. Tony's business was an overnight success.[33] The
public, when given the option of purchasing slave-free chocolate,
responded with enthusiasm. The solution wasn't to abandon chocolate farmers and stop buying chocolate altogether, but they sent
the message with their money that they would support oppression-
free chocolate. Tony also continues his fight to help the cocoa
farmers and end the terror of slavery by raising awareness.
Through television specials and a planned documentary, *Tony and
the Slave-Free Chocolate Factory,* he hopes to get more consumers
to insist on slave-free chocolate. For Tony, chocolate production is

a moral issue that will only change if enough people choose to opt out of an oppressive system.

In my own life, seeking out slave-free chocolate is the easy route to follow. I enjoy the treat of a good piece of dark chocolate and further enjoy knowing that I can support slave-free practices with my purchase. I do my best to tell others about slave-free options and choose to personally serve only those options. And yes, I've handed out slave-free pirate gold on Halloween! But I am not legalistic about chocolate. If I'm offered a slice of chocolate cake or given a box of chocolates, I won't insult the giver by saying "I can't eat this because I don't know if it is slave-free." I do my best to care for these children and seek change while still showing love to those around me. Seeking justice and respecting the image of God in everyone requires knowing when to speak up and when to gracefully stay silent. The point is this: *for change to occur and for the cries of these slave children to be heard, enough people need to speak up.* This can involve activism, writing letters or simply altering our shopping habits—but it does require doing something. It's up to you to decide what that something will be in your own life.

FOR MORE INFORMATION

Books

Bales, Kevin. *Disposable People: New Slavery in the Global Economy.* Berkeley: University of California Press, 1999. An overview of modern slavery that details the causes, tells stories about slavery in various countries and proposes possible solutions.

Batstone, David. *Not for Sale: The Return of the Global Slave Trade— and How We Can Fight It.* New York: HarperCollins, 2007. An inspiring look at modern-day abolitionists and the campaign to end human bondage.

Hunter, Zach. *Be the Change: Your Guide to Freeing Slaves and Changing the World.* Grand Rapids: Zondervan, 2007. A youth-oriented action guide for ending modern-day slavery.

Metaxas, Eric. *Amazing Grace: William Wilberforce and the Heroic Campaign to End Slavery.* New York: HarperCollins, 2007. A historic look at the nineteenth-century abolitionists.

Off, Carol. *Bitter Chocolate: The Dark Side of the World's Most Seductive Sweet.* New York: The New Press, 2006. A detailed history of chocolate and its long connection to slavery.

Movies

Amazing Grace. Directed by Michael Apted. 117 min., 20th Century Fox, 2007. A dramatic retelling of William Wilberforce's campaign to end the slave trade in England.

Call+Response. Produced and directed by Justin Dillon. 86 min., Fair Trade Pictures, 2008. An overview of modern-day slavery that uses music to send out the call for action, a call to which we must respond.

The Price of Sugar. Directed by Bill Haney. 90 min., New Yorker Video, 2007. A documentary looking at the slavelike conditions many Haitians experience in the sugar fields.

Websites

Stop the Traffik
www.stopthetraffik.org
A global movement against trafficking people

Stop Chocolate Slavery
http://vision.ucsd.edu/~kbranson/stopchocolateslavery/good
chocolateproducts.html
Helps raise awareness about slavery and chocolate, while encouraging and facilitating actions aimed at ending abuses

International Justice Mission
www.ijm.org
An organization that seeks legal justice for the victims of modern-day slavery

3

Cars

THE GLOBAL AND LOCAL IMPACT
OF OIL CONSUMPTION

Megan was getting anxious. The gas light was on again, and they still had a long way to drive before they got home. While Emily chatted away in the backseat, as toddlers always do, Megan began to look around for gas stations. She hated filling up the Aztek. Just watching those numbers climb was enough to ruin her day. Who ever thought she'd be paying $4.29 for gas, and it just hurt all the worse when she had to fill up the SUV.

They'd considered getting a smaller car that didn't make such a dent in their bank account, but this one was paid off and there was no way they could afford a new car payment. She envied her friend who had just bought a Prius, wondering how often she had to fill up. Sure her car was environmentally friendly, but it was way out of the range of Megan's budget. Besides, Megan didn't think she was ready to give up all the cargo space quite yet. Every cubic inch of her car got crammed full of stuff on a regular basis between sports events, camping trips and visits to the grandparents (with the mountains of stuff required to travel with a toddler). That space was rather useful.

The gas light blinked at her again. Megan looked harder for a gas station.

"Mommy, what are you doing?" Emily asked from the backseat.

"I'm looking for a gas station, honey," Megan replied, distracted.

"But Mommy, we just passed one."

Megan sighed. They had just passed a BP, and stopping there would have been very convenient, but she just couldn't do it. She replied to Emily, "I know sweetie, but I'm trying not to go to those stations."

"Why?"

"Well, because I read in the paper that their local plant is dumping unsafe levels of mercury into Lake Michigan, and they are trying to get the laws changed so they can continue dumping those chemicals into the lake. That's where we go swimming and get our drinking water from, and I don't want any yucky chemicals floating around our lake. So I don't want to support what they are doing by buying gas from them," Megan explained, not really expecting Emily to understand most of what she had just said.[1]

"So how will we make the car go to get me to dance class?" Emily asked, grasping that gas made cars go.

"Oh, there are lots of other gas stations out there," Megan replied. "Look, I see a Chevron up ahead. Their commercials say they're trying to take care of the environment, so we might as well buy gas from them."[2]

☛

During 2008 I got in the habit of taking pictures of gas-station price signs. During the spring and summer, as gas prices climbed well over the four-dollar mark, one station near my home displayed on their sign "Regular Unleaded: An Arm and a Leg." I also had to photographically document the time, later that fall, when gas dropped under two dollars a gallon for the first time in over three years. This roller coaster of gas prices had many of us rethinking our reliance on traditional gasoline, but it also helped open my eyes to the worldwide implications of our addiction to oil.

Beyond the strain on our pocketbooks, the effects of our oil usage are far more complex and far-reaching than we could ever dream. Oil consumption in the form of gasoline affects the world with the pollution it creates, but the production of that oil in the first place also has serious consequences. Oil is, in many ways, tied to global injustice.

CLIMATE CHANGE AND ENERGY USAGE

If I had to name the one justice issue that gets the most press these days, it would be climate change (also somewhat misleadingly known as global warming). In recent years the dialogue surrounding this issue has permeated our social consciousness, with conversation centerpieces like former vice president Al Gore's movie, *An Inconvenient Truth* (his campaign to educate the public about climate change even earned him the Nobel Peace Prize). I am aware, of course, of the debates surrounding the entire climate-change issue. It is far beyond the scope of this book to address all those concerns here. Our understanding of our world and science is always evolving, but as the data pours in, the vast majority of scientists affirm the realities and dangers of climate change.[3] But beyond the debates, there are few who would deny the need to care for God's creation. We have scarred the earth and its people with our abuse of resources, and we should do our part to bring healing to those wounds. Media reports of supposed scientific uncertainty about climate change shouldn't encourage us to throw caution to the wind and continue to harm the earth, but they should instead temper us to more careful and thoughtful action. Unfortunately, amidst the controversy and media hype, it is sometimes difficult to understand what's actually happening and how we can best respond.

Simply put, climate change refers to the effects greenhouse gases have on our atmosphere, effects that cause the earth's average temperature to rise. Burning fossil fuels like oil produce these greenhouse gases (including carbon dioxide). Brought on by the advent of industrialization, the use of fossil fuels has steadily increased as the world's population has grown. In the United States (the world's largest oil consumer) about 20 percent of carbon dioxide emissions comes from cars and light trucks, and another 40 percent comes from burning fossil fuels for the purpose of generating electricity.[4] Our reliance on cars and fossil-fuel energy is a major factor in the climate-change crisis.

CLIMATE CHANGE: the effects of greenhouse gases on the earth's long-term average temperature.

What will this crisis involve? Altering earth's average temperature just a couple of degrees will have far-reaching consequences. Among other things, scientists predict sea levels will rise, drowning many low lying areas and displacing millions of people and animals who call those areas home, and also leading to the extinction of numerous species. It will also diminish natural resources like glaciers. For instance, ecologists predict that by 2030 there will be no more glaciers in Glacier National Park.[5] Glaciers provide much of earth's fresh water, and as water becomes scarcer around the world, agricultural yields will be drastically affected, and drought will become more common in previously fertile regions. We are already seeing some of these effects worldwide, and people are literally starving because they don't have access to sufficient food and water.

Climate change is also expected to increase the intensity of extreme weather like hurricanes. As already seen in New Orleans and the Gulf Coast in 2005, severe storms have the potential to destroy communities and scatter people seeking refuge around the globe. Rising sea levels and strange new weather patterns have already altered the ecosystem in parts of Bangladesh, forcing thousands of "climate refugees" to flee to India. Some estimate that, within this century, over a quarter of Bangladesh will be underwater and 30 to 40 million people displaced.[6] That is a high cost to pay for a traditional fisherman or rice farmer who has never used fossil fuels in his life, and all so that we can continue to fill up our SUVs.

Some reports even predict that entire islands in the Pacific could be devastated as sea levels rise due to climate change. In 2002 the small island of Tuvalu started recruiting other Pacific nations to join a planned lawsuit against the United States and Australia (two of the world's largest polluters) for the destruction of their homes.[7] A mere eight-inch sea-level rise would drown the island, and even a few inches could destroy the soil and groundwater. Worse yet, climate change from pollution has the potential to cause sea levels to rise much more than that! While this small nation of 10,000 is fighting a giant, I find myself wishing that they didn't feel the need to bring this to a fight at all. I'd like to believe that, if the people in the United States were aware of how our actions were hurting others, we would choose to love our neighbors and take the steps to reduce pollution and stop the negative consequences of climate change. So far, however, countries like Tuvalu are only perceiving the message that we don't value their survival (since they don't see us making changes) and thus feel that a lawsuit may be their only recourse.

Real lives are affected by our use of gas and oil, and the people it affects are people God commands us to love and respect as his image bearers. Their lives are important, and demand our love and attention. For them, climate change isn't a theory to be debated but a disaster threatening their very survival. If we are to act justly on their behalf, we need to rethink our consumption of gas and oil.

However, I must admit that, at times, it can be difficult to really wrap our minds around the ways something like climate change actually affects our lives. It seems so future-oriented, and the media controversy that still surrounds it doesn't help us focus on the practicalities of our gas consumption. Beyond long-term climate issues, though, the current development of oil resources is already affecting the world and the people in it. Oil companies are inflicting serious damage in localized environments, affecting the people living in those areas. These actions ruin lives and treat people more often as objects to be brushed aside if they get in the way of making money rather than as the reflections of God's image that they are. Seeking justice in these situations is necessary to help restore their lives.

LOVING OUR LOCAL NEIGHBORS

Megan's predicament as to where she should buy gas was a very real problem for Chicago-area residents during the summer of 2007. Local newspapers reported that a BP refinery in nearby Indiana received an exemption on its new state water permit to bypass federal guidelines regarding the amount of mercury it could dump into Lake Michigan. Although the federal guidelines were put in place over a decade before, the exemption gave BP until at least 2012 to comply.[8]

This refinery dumps over two pounds of mercury into the lake every year. While this may seem like a small amount, to put it in perspective, if BP were to meet federal standards, it would take the refinery twenty-five years to put the same amount of the toxic metal into Lake Michigan! While Lake Michigan is a pretty big lake (it is a "Great Lake," after all), over time, mercury builds up in an environment and is so toxic that even small amounts can harm or even kill fish and people. As a neurotoxin, mercury can cause debilitating effects in adults and can cause severe brain damage in fetuses if a pregnant mother is exposed to mercury in the environment or consumes tainted fish.[9]

Since Lake Michigan serves as a major draw for leisure activities like fishing, boating and swimming, and also provides most of the drinking water for the Chicago area, you can imagine how people reacted when this news hit the stands. Environmental groups spoke out on the impact of mercury on the environment and human health, while concerned citizens sent thousands of letters and made calls to BP asking them to stop polluting the lake. Besides these letters and phone calls, many of the citizens of Chicago also chose to boycott BP gas stations. They sent the message with words and deeds: Stop polluting our water and endangering our lives just so you can save a little money.

This issue pitted the objectives of a company—to make a profit—against the health and well-being of people. Both individuals and whole communities were not being treated with dignity and respect, nor were they being loved as image bearers of God. The refinery seemed to assume that the well-being of their bottom line justified killing fish, closing beaches and potentially damaging babies. I understand how it is difficult for companies to do the right thing and also protect their bottom line. Refinery managers have strict budgets to stick to and shareholders are expecting to make a profit. But short-term constraints and turning a profit don't excuse harming the earth and its people. Of course BP isn't the only company to have ever made that sort of value judgment (choosing profits over people), but they were the ones that caused a city to stand up and say "what you are doing is not right, and we will do our best to stop you." All of a sudden, for thousands of Chicago-area residents, buying gas became not just a private act, but a question of justice for an entire region.

Within a month of the story breaking, BP announced that it would begin to voluntarily comply with federal pollution standards. While it remains to be seen if they will make good on their promise (they have since claimed to be unsure whether it is even possible),[10] the voice of the people pushed for change and saw results. Acting justly was as easy as making a phone call, writing a letter and driving to a different gas station. But it required someone to be willing to tell the story of injustice, others to spread the word and still others to be moved enough to actually do something. "Doing something" doesn't have to be big or dramatic; sometimes it can be simple steps that help make life better for the neighbors Jesus instructed us to love.

Unfortunately sometimes we don't always know when our neighbor is suffering from injustice. The BP story made the news and captured attention because it had local impact. But we can't forget that our local decisions can affect our neighbors around the world as well.

LOVING OUR GLOBAL NEIGHBORS

In choosing to love her local neighbors by not giving her support to BP, Megan chose instead to buy gas at Chevron. Their television commercials portrayed them as a forward-thinking company seeking alternative fuel solutions to help reduce our reliance on conventional oil. While commending that approach for the company, Chevron's history holds injustices as well.

Nigeria is the world's fifth largest oil producer, providing oil for companies like Chevron. In the days of colonial expansion, the British Empire formed Nigeria from pieces of four independent kingdoms, but they did it through violent means. After Nigeria gained independence from Great Britain in 1960, the remains of those ancient tribal kingdoms vied for power and survival. A series of dictators made themselves rich by selling land that belonged to other tribes—but contained newfound oil reserves—to large, multinational companies. These companies (Shell and Chevron, to name a few) often supported the military regimes of these dictators and have since been implicated in the deaths of activists who opposed their actions.[11] These oil companies devastated natural environments and often (with government aid) forced these native people to relocate off oil-rich lands.

In the 1990s protest groups formed to speak out against the rape of the land by the oil companies. The early protests of these injustices, mostly led by women, were peaceful, focusing on diplomacy and discussion. These women, who lived by fishing the Niger River Delta the way their ancestors had before them, had much to protest. When Chevron-Texaco wanted to build oil-drilling and processing plants right in the delta, they didn't bother to ask permission from the local women who lived off that land. Instead they arranged things with corrupt government officials and simply took it. They built walled and gated compounds, brought in their own workers and refused to hire local men, and the local men soon found out that if they protested for jobs, the hired military would show up and beat them down—or even kill them.

Chemical and oil spills harmed the women's fishing economy, and oil flares caused acid rain, which destroyed the roofs of their houses and led to skin diseases and asthma, among other things. The environmental damage to the river delta caused by the oil companies even caused some of the villages to start sinking as the ecosystem adjusted to the ravages imposed on it. The women soon found it impossible to continue in the way of life they had always known. As one mother explained, "In the past our mothers were into fishing from w[h]ere they were able to train their children. But now that the oil companies have come, we cannot go fishing again."[12]

In June 2002, a group of women decided to complain to Chevron-Texaco. The oil company's response came quickly: mercenary soldiers tortured the women and burned their fishing boats.[13] The women, a few hundred strong, then gathered from around the Niger Delta to stage a peaceful protest in July of that year. They slipped into the main processing plant and blocked the pump stations and roads and runways. As one woman explained their action, "The Federal government and the oil companies know what they should do, but they like to oppress us. Since we are already suffering, we did not mind if we died in the flow stations."[14]

The women had five demands:

- The oil companies should stop killing their sons for peacefully protesting for the right to work and have jobs.

- The pollution of farms and rivers should end, and a clean-up process begin immediately.

- The oil companies should respect local customs and traditions by negotiating with the traditional leaders and elders.

- They should provide clean water, electricity, health care and free education in exchange for taking the land.

- The local people should have the right to live in peace in their homeland, away from military and political violence.[15]

This protest involved women of all ages standing together as one. But their songs and peaceful protest were met, as one woman described it,

> with vehicles filled with soldiers and penetration fire and policemen who immediately started beating, torturing and flogging us with horsewhips, guns and boots. Several canisters of tear-gas were fired at us, at close range, some of us ran into the bush. And the soldiers and policemen pursued us into the bush and water. At the end of the exercise the staff hospitalized at least 2 persons who were beaten into coma and several others were hospitalized in other various places that evening. As we speak, 2 women have not been found. Only their wrappers were seen floating on the river.[16]

Even in the face of this violence, the women didn't give up.

They returned with a threat of their own—one that would bring the most shame, according to the norms of that culture, to the men involved. They threatened to strip.[17] As Westerners, we might have a hard time understanding a culture where seeing a woman's naked body is more shameful than beating her into a coma, but the threat worked. Chevron agreed to the demands and started working to improve the conditions of the lives they ruined.[18] Things aren't perfect, but they are better than they were because the women came together to put their lives on the line, raise their voices against injustice and help create a better world for their families.

It may be hard to fathom, but the story of these women in Nigeria is part of a global system that we also participate in when we fill up our cars with gas. As Megan chose one gas station over another, she made a value judgment about which company's ethical standards she would support. We are in a similar position of voting for a company's morality whenever we make purchases. Whether we are aware of the issues or not, when we give money to a company we implicitly tell them that we approve of their corporate practices, including how they treat their employees, local communities and the environment. Even so, being constantly aware of the ethical implications of our actions, much less finding out information about different companies ahead of time, is difficult. And even if some of us want to act justly, most of us cannot just stop using gas and other oil-based products.

This story of the Niger Delta women reminded me, however, of another story where enacting justice also seemed hopeless. First Kings 21 contains the story of Naboth's vineyard. It takes place during the reign of the infamous King Ahab and his wife Jezebel, who established pagan practices in Israel and called for the death of God's prophet Elijah. As the story goes, Ahab decided that he liked some land owned by a man named Naboth, and he wanted it for himself. He offered to buy it, but Naboth refused to sell the land of his ancestors. Ahab went home and pouted about it to his wife Jezebel. Annoyed at Ahab's pouting, she determined to get him what he desired. Jezebel brought false accusations against Naboth, and he was subsequently stoned to death, allowing Ahab to seize the land for himself. Just like the oil companies who seized the land from the Nigerian people to meet their own needs, the powerful Ahab and Jezebel trampled on the poor and powerless and took for themselves.

After this unjust murder and seizure of land, God called his prophet Elijah to go and confront the king. Elijah told Ahab, "You have sold yourself to do evil in the eyes of the LORD. [The LORD] says, 'I am going to bring disaster on you'" (1 Kings 21:20-21). Elijah went on to detail to him his own death and the death of his wife as the consequences of their unjust actions. Somewhat surprisingly, these words from God's prophet hit Ahab hard. His response was to tear his clothes, put on sackcloth and fast. It took Elijah delivering the message that what they had done was unjust, and that God and others knew about it, for Ahab to admit his wrongdoing.

Likewise, in our world today it takes people willing to stand up and say "This isn't right" when they see injustice. Elijah was the one who brought that message to Ahab, but it took entire groups of people to say those words to BP and Chevron. The voice of the community had to come together around a common goal of seeking justice to bring about change. It's important to remember that, even when we feel like one voice won't make much of a difference, by joining with others and spreading the word we can effect great change.

Everyday justice begins with staying informed about what is happening to our neighbors around the world.

Practically speaking, this can involve making phone calls or writing letters or e-mails to companies involved in unjust acts. It might also mean not giving your money to a certain company for a period of time. But whatever the steps, acting justly requires staying informed. Read the paper and watch the news to become aware of what is going on around you. Unfortunately, however, mainstream American media doesn't often report on the ongoing injustices around the world. I find it helpful to seek out foreign news sources, like the BBC, or independent news groups, like *Democracy Now!,* to broaden my exposure to world events. Encourage your local media to report on such things or even write editorials yourself to spread the word. If we are to love our neighbors around the world, we need to know what is going on in their lives.

LOVING THE CREATION AND ITS INHABITANTS

Beyond becoming more informed, however, practicing justice in this area will ultimately have to mean changing our habits to reduce our reliance on gas and oil products. The following list provides some ways to get started in reducing our consumption of oil. Some of these involve major lifestyle changes and some are small tweaks. Some might not be possible at all for you right now, but others might be the perfect place to begin.

Ways to reduce our gas consumption.
Drive less. This may sound like a no-brainer, but it is the most effective way to reduce gas consumption. If the weather permits, walk or ride bikes for local errands. Form carpools for the commute to work or for children's activities. Take advantage of your city's mass transit system whenever possible. Plan any outing ahead of time to make the most efficient use of fuel. Combine errands to reduce total driving time. Plan weekly shopping needs in order to make one economical trip instead of a half-dozen shorter ones.

Make cars fuel-efficient. This could involve purchasing a fuel-efficient car like a hybrid or one that runs on biodiesel, but it also involves making sure your car is properly maintained. Keep tires properly inflated so the engine doesn't have to work harder and burn more gas. Replace air filters at the proper times and keep the spark plugs clean to reduce gas consumption in any car. And get the useless junk out of the car: the heavier the car, the more gas it uses.

Reduce the amount of plastic we use. Plastic is made from oil, and our world seems to have an obsession with plastic. But to make the nearly fifty billion plastic bottles we buy each year, it takes as much oil as it does to fuel one million cars for an entire year—and that is just the oil used in the bottles themselves, not counting manufacturing and transportation expenditures.[19] We can easily reduce our part in that waste by only using reusable water bottles.

Change our eating habits. In America, food typically travels over 1,500 miles to get to our table. That's a lot of gas. Buy locally produced food whenever possible. Similarly, buying organic foods will reduce oil consumption. Nonorganic foods are sprayed with pesticides that are oil based. Given both of these factors, recent research shows that approximately ten calories of fossil fuels are required to produce every one calorie of food eaten in the United States.[20] In choosing to eat local, organic foods that use less fossil fuels to produce, we can reduce our oil consumption.

Control the temperature of our homes. Turn down the thermostat in the winter, and turn it up in the summer. For every degree we lower the thermostat in the winter, we can cut energy use by about 3 percent. And make sure the ducts in your home are sealed. Sealing the ducts and insulating the portions that pass through unconditioned spaces—such as the attic, basement or garage—can reduce carbon dioxide emissions, and heating and cooling costs, by up to 40 percent.

Use energy-efficient appliances. Many appliances are available in energy-efficient models, so if you are in the market for a new appliance, look for energy-efficient ones. You can make the biggest difference by getting an energy-efficient water heater. And with any appliance (even cell phone chargers), unplug it when it is not in use to prevent it from draining energy, which can happen even when turned "off." Finally, install compact fluorescent light bulbs (CFLs) to save energy, but be sure to properly dispose of them since they do contain mercury.

Simplify. Let go of the busyness and the need to always be on the move. Reduce the amount of places we drive to, and spend more time with our family and neighbors. Stop buying things we don't really need. Don't get the huge house that uses a ton of energy to heat or cool. Reuse things and shop at resale shops. We can grow food for our families and get to know local farmers. Changing how we live will have a huge impact on the amount of oil and gas we consume. It may be difficult, but our children and grandchildren (and the children in Nigeria and Tuvalu) will thank us for it.

Lobby to seek alternative fuel options. Beyond reducing our oil consumption, we can seek out alternative fuel options. Biofuel technology is expanding, creating cleaner fuels from crops like corn and soy, as well as seaweed and algae. Wind, geothermal and solar solutions are also on the rise. These options have the potential to give us cleaner energy, but unfortunately, they often cost more to install than the average person can afford. Choosing to use these alternatives when we can is an everyday step we can take, but many believe that it will take government subsidies for these to become viable, widespread alternatives in the United States. Many European nations are already subsidizing alternative fuel options. Iceland and Sweden pledge to be petroleum free by midcentury, and that task is well underway. Asking our elected officials to follow those countries' examples is a simple way we can take a stand for justice for all.

EVERYDAY PRACTITIONER

David Radcliff, director,
New Community Project, Elgin, Illinois

In 2003 David Radcliff gave up his car. For several years he had been increasing his bicycle usage as a means of local transportation, and he finally decided to give up having a personal car. His deep concern for the environment was at the heart of his decision. He knew driving was his biggest personal, environmental impact, so he opted for a means of transportation that won't contribute to pollution. He understands that radical changes are necessary to reduce the effects of our oil usage, and he knows that those changes have to originate with individual people. For him, that choice was to switch to riding a bike.

Besides the impact of gasoline usage on the environment, David has personally witnessed the damaging effects oil drilling has on communities around the world. As he led tours of the Ecuadorian Amazon, he saw how oil drilling caused the destruction of native communities. And he's made friends with the Gwich'in people near the Arctic National Wildlife Refuge who oppose the continued push to drill for oil there. They have lived as "caribou people" for ten thousand years, and oil drilling would affect the caribou population and thus their way of life. When David decided that he couldn't justify contributing to the destruction of others' way of life by driving a car, he chose to follow Jesus' call to love our neighbors.

The environment and the world's poor, who are most affected by the environmental harm caused by oil usage, often do not have a voice within the global system. David tries to care for the environment and these people by giving them a voice, and by doing his part to avoid the systems that harm them. Doing so is simply part of his Christian faith—choosing to follow and obey Jesus. He realizes that not everyone is able to give up driving a car, but since it was a feasible option for him, he made that choice. He enjoys the health benefits bike riding offers and likes serving as one of the more uncommon examples of ways people can reduce their oil usage. As he sees it, since individuals have contributed to messing up the planet, it is up to each of us to find solutions to make amends.[21]

For more information about David's work to help the environment visit <www.newcommunityproject.org>.

CONCLUSION

Of course, it will take time and effort to implement these steps consistently into our life. For me, certain things were easy, like installing compact fluorescent light bulbs and planting a garden. I've looked into adding solar panels to my house but am still exploring that option. Changing my driving habits proved the most difficult though. Megan's scenario at the start of this chapter was a fairly autobiographical one. I, too, drive a paid-off Aztek—a car with an identity problem of, alternately, being labeled a large station wagon or a small SUV—and let's just say that it isn't the most gas-efficient mode of transportation out there. I have all sorts of excuses as to why I need the extra space—including not having had to rent a trailer for our church plant or for my craft business—but even amidst my justifications, I knew I had to make changes. So, never having been one to plan ahead with my errands, I started to force myself to plan in advance and limit my driving. Honestly, it didn't take long to make a habit of it. And even though, in the past, I've lived in areas where there is no public transportation, I found that a number of places I frequented were within walking distance. Still, I had to force myself to take the time and energy to walk when and where I could. I still don't do it often enough, but I am getting better (although this native Texan had issues with bundling up and pushing the stroller through the snow in a Chicago January to get to the grocery store!). For longer distances I try to arrange carpooling. It isn't always possible, but even the hassle of the extra phone call or shuffling car seats around is worth reducing my impact on the environment and my reliance on oil.

I'm also encouraged by the examples of others who've chosen to make small changes that have resulted in big differences. The shipping giant UPS, for instance, decided to stop making left-hand turns. Seriously. Sitting in an idle vehicle waiting to make a left-hand turn wastes gas. Take nearly 95,000 trucks delivering packages each day and the wasted gas adds up fast. So UPS decided to carefully plan their delivery routes to eliminate as many left-hand turns as possible. The result? In 2006 this planning helped UPS cut 28.5 million miles off its delivery routes and saved them roughly, 3 million gallons of gas, reducing carbon dioxide emissions by 31,000 metric tons.[22] Small changes in our everyday actions *do* add up and make a difference if enough of us start doing them. But we each have to do our part.

FOR MORE INFORMATION

Books

Bouma-Prediger, Steven. *For the Beauty of the Earth: A Christian Vision for Creation Care.* Grand Rapids: Baker Academic, 2001. An overview of the Christian responsibility and privilege of being stewards of God's creation.

Lowe, Ben. *Green Revolution: Coming Together to Care for Creation.* Downers Grove, Ill.: IVP Books, 2009. An exploration of the environment crisis and suggestions for sustainable living.

Manby, Bronwen. *The Price of Oil: Corporate Responsibility and Human Rights Violations in Nigeria's Oil Producing Communities.* New York: Human Rights Watch, 1999. A political report on the oil crisis in Nigeria.

Reay, Dave. *Climate Change Begins at Home.* New York: Macmillan, 2005. An exploration of the impact of the typical American, suburban family on the environment and the significant lifestyle changes they need to make to reduce their negative impact.

Movies

The 11th Hour. Directed by Nadia Conners and Leila Conners Peterson. 92 min., Warner Home Video, 2007. An exploration of the causes of global warming and everyday suggestions of what we can do to stop it.

Fuel. Directed by Josh Tickell. 112 min., Blue Water Entertainment, 2008. A hopeful overview of alternative fuel sources.

An Inconvenient Truth. Directed by Davis Guggenheim. 96 min., Paramount, 2006. Al Gore's award-winning documentary on the global climate crisis and suggestions for a sustainable future.

Who Killed the Electric Car? Directed by Chris Paine. 93 min., Sony Pictures, 2006. A look at the economic and political barriers to creating alternative-fuel vehicles.

Websites

Evangelical Environmental Network
www.creationcare.org
Encourages Christians to worship God and love his people by caring for his creation

Environmental Protection Agency—Climate Change
www.epa.gov/climatechange
Resources for understanding global warming and practical suggestions for what you can do to stop it

Greener Choices
www.greenerchoices.org
Consumer Reports' guide to lifestyle changes that help reduce our environmental impact and help save money

Carbon Footprint
www.carbonfootprint.com
A resource that calculates your carbon footprint (how much energy you use), with suggestions for how you can reduce and offset that footprint

$$\binom{4}{}$$

Food

CHOOSING TO EAT ETHICALLY

Chris stared at the table in front of him, not entirely sure what he was doing.

Over the past year, Chris's wife, Amy, had started researching healthy and sustainable eating habits. She read dozens of books and had slowly begun to change their diet. She, of course, tried to explain it all to Chris but very little sunk in. To him, food was food. He'd heard that "local" and "organic" were good things, but he had no idea why. For the most part, he just let Amy make all those decisions—which was why he was now standing in front of a table at the local farmers' market feeling like a complete idiot.

"Lettuce," Amy said. "Can you find us some lettuce for a salad tonight?"

Then she walked off to peruse some locally made cheeses, leaving Chris to fend for himself on the Great Lettuce Hunt.

He didn't expect it to be so difficult. Arrayed before him on the table were about a dozen different sorts of leafy greens, and not a one looked like the round ball of iceberg lettuce he was accustomed to buying. He didn't even know if some of this stuff was lettuce.

"Can I help you?" asked the young girl in blue jeans behind the table.

"Um, I'm looking for some lettuce," Chris replied.

"Okay, any particular type?"

"Salad lettuce?" Chris responded hopefully.

"No problem. These six here are perfect for salads and are great if you combine them. We should be getting more varieties in next week as they come into season," the girl replied helpfully.

"Lettuce has a season?" Chris asked skeptically. "I thought it just always grew; I mean we eat it all year round."

"Well, I bet you don't eat anything that tastes as good as this stuff all year long," the girl replied with pride. "This stuff is locally grown, picked from our fields this morning. It hasn't been treated with chemicals or preserved in unnatural temperatures. Nope, just treated to the Wilson-family love."

"So your whole family helps grow this?" Chris asked.

"Yep, the whole family. We have a farm just a half-hour outside of town, where we grow our own food that's healthy and doesn't harm the Earth. It's my job to get up at 5 a.m. to feed the chickens."

"Wow," Chris replied. "That's committed. I'm just the guy who's overwhelmed by the fact that there are so many types of lettuce out there. My wife's the one who knows all about stuff like this."

"Well you gotta start somewhere," the girl said with a smile. "And lettuce is a good place to start since you have the whole season ahead of you to discover what good food is actually like. We're here every week, with something new each time. If you get here early enough, I generally bring eggs from my chickens as well."

"I don't know about the getting here early part," Chris laughed as he paid for his lettuce. "I like sleeping in, but I'm interested in seeing how the season unfolds. Maybe I'll even learn something about the food I eat."

"Sounds good. Enjoy the lettuce."

"Will do," Chris replied as he wandered off to find his wife.

In the fall of 2008, I read with horror the reports of hundreds of thousands of babies in China falling ill due to melamine poisoning. Baby-formula manufacturers had laced their formula with the chemical to help it appear to have a higher protein content. Melamine can cause kidney and bladder problems—potentially even kidney failure. Six babies in China died from this contamination. Reports then surfaced that the same chemical is found in some infant formulas in the United States (though in far smaller amounts), apparently due to cleaning-product residue on formula-manufacturing machines.

Around this same time my infant son's doctor advised me not to make him baby food from conventionally grown carrots. The overuse of fertilizers in growing produce like carrots results in high nitrate levels that can be potentially fatal to babies (inhibiting oxygen absorption in the bloodstream and leading to asphyxiation). As a mother, these reports infuriated me. *How can we justify the presence of poison in our food, much less feed such poison to our* children? But even as I asked such a question, I knew that contaminants in baby food are simply the tip of the proverbial iceberg when it comes to problems with food.

"You are what you eat" is a common refrain used to promote healthy eating habits. Just look at a magazine rack and you'll notice our obsession with food. We want to know how we can eat the foods we love and still lose weight. We nitpick over fat content, calories and nutrients. We follow the latest celebrity chefs but seek shortcuts to creating quick and easy meals. Food, or at least our immediate relationship to it, is often on our minds.

Apart from food-contamination scandals like the melamine in baby formula, we rarely examine the impact our food choices have on the world around us. How often do we ask questions like "Was this sustainably produced?" "Did the production of this food harm people or the environment?" "Where was this food grown, and were the workers who grew it paid fair wages?" or "How far did this food travel to get to my table?" These questions open our eyes to the ethical issues involved with our food choices. "You are what you eat" takes on a deeper meaning when we realize that the story of our food is much bigger than what we typically assume.

At the most basic level is the question of how the food we eat was grown. As awareness of the issues surrounding food make their way into public consciousness, we hear terms like *conventionally* or *organically grown* thrown around. While conventional methods employ the use of chemical pesticides and artificial fertilizers, organic produce is free from those and any other industrial-waste contamination. The irony here is that, before the last century or so (and in much of the world today), what is labeled "organic" *was* the conventional option. Only in modern times have genetically engineered foods—sprayed with all sorts of fertilizers and pesticides, or crowded into factory farms that feed animals unnatural diets and pump them full of antibiotics and hormones—become the norm.

SUSTAINABILITY: using earth's resources at a rate at which they can be replenished.

While shopping with my preschool-age daughter one day, she asked me why I sought to purchase organic food options. I explained to her that organic food doesn't require the use of nasty chemicals that harm our health, the people who grow our food or the earth. Incredulous, she wondered why anyone would ever want to use the nasty chemicals if they do such awful things. Her young question is worth considering. How did such scientifically altered, environmentally hazardous and technologically dependent methods become the standard while age-old sustainable practices are now labeled as "new," "trendy" or "elitist"?

To answer that question, let's take a peek at the story behind two common foods in America. In understanding where these foods come from and the bigger picture they represent, I hope we can begin to consider the ethical issues connected to our food choices.

THE ISSUES WITH OUR FOOD

The ethical problems with our modern food-production system stem from the fact that this system often harms people, animals and the environment. Food is not just food. What we eat involves history, economics and politics. It touches the lives of farmers, communities and corporations. While it would be nice to believe that a farmer grows a crop, sells it to the local market for a decent price and feeds the families in his area, that is rarely the case. Instead, decisions are made by the government or CEOs, who set the rules for modern farming. Governments subsidize certain crops (like corn or soy), but they often require that farmers receiving subsidies not grow any other food (even in personal gardens!). Agribusinesses, which control vast amounts of the production of certain crops, have the power and the money to market their produce worldwide, often putting smaller farmers out of business. The food we eat no longer comes fresh from the farm, and it is often modified with chemicals, hormones or antibiotics. Furthermore, the workers who provide our food often face exploitation and oppression. Yet the average consumer knows little about any of this. To illustrate these issues, I bring you the stories of tomatoes and cheeseburgers.

Tomatoes. Growing up I refused to eat tomatoes. I found everything about them repulsive—the taste, the texture, their tendency to show up everywhere. So a few years ago when I joined a local CSA (Community Supported Agriculture) farm, I dreaded the advent of tomato season. In CSA, a person buys a share in a local farm and then receives weekly produce from that farm. It's a way of directly supporting local farmers and reaping the benefits (or suffering the losses) of the harvest.

Having signed up to share in one farm's bounty for a season, I found that the bounty included tomatoes—*lots* of tomatoes. Not wanting to waste food, I geared myself up to endure the dreaded food. But what I discovered in my weekly produce box were a variety of oddly shaped and strangely colored tomatoes that tasted amazing. What were these delectable globes of goodness seemingly masquerading as tomatoes!? They were heirloom tomatoes allowed to ripen on the vine—ah, tomatoes as they were meant to be, apart from the mass-produced, grocery-store variety most of us think of. I discovered that I actually like tomatoes.

Yet I soon realized that the issues with tomatoes (as with much of the produce we eat) are far more complex than how they taste. A tomato is never just a tomato; it represents a long story, one full of environmental destruction, oppression of workers, slavery and competing worldviews. That may sound a bit melodramatic, but the story of what we eat is far from straightforward.

The reason I had never tasted a good tomato before is because most grocery stores limit the variety of tomatoes they sell—for ease in transport, storage and display. For tomatoes to be available throughout the year (as opposed to when they are in season), they must be grown around the world and then shipped to your local grocery store. This requires tomatoes that can survive long distances. Most ripe produce goes bad after a few days, and transporting it leaves bruises on the flesh. The solution to these "problems" involves growing a very limited variety of tomatoes that can withstand travel, then picking them before they are ripe, transporting them hundreds of miles in refrigerated crates and artificially "ripening" them (changing the color but not really ripening) with ethylene gas. The result: using vast amounts of oil and energy to get perfect-looking, red-ball tomatoes, which don't taste like much of anything, to your table in January.

Other varieties that aren't bred for such abuse (the ones that need to ripen on the vine and don't refrigerate or travel well) have slowly passed out of public awareness and consumption. The variety of tomatoes that we now call "heirlooms" can only be found these days in farmers' markets, CSAs and the occasional health-food store. In the name of food on demand, all year around, we not only sacrifice the diverse bounty of God's creation and the wonders of taste it provides, but we also ignore how unnatural it may be and the toll it takes on the Earth to transport food (an energy source) by using vast amounts of other energy.

Many of the tomatoes we get during the winter months are grown in sunny Florida and then shipped across the country.[1] Unfortunately, to keep consumer prices low on well-traveled food, farm owners often pass on the hidden costs to their workers. The tomatoes that end up in our homes and fast-food restaurants are picked by people who typically live and work in deplorable conditions and receive substandard wages. Most of the tomato pickers in Florida are migrant workers (both legal and illegal) from Latin America and Haiti who are trying to survive and support their families in their native homelands. Yet the jobs that they are able to find are oftentimes barely jobs at all. They soon discover that, to get a job picking tomatoes, they must live on and buy food from those very farms where unscrupulous supervisors charge them exorbitantly for food or rent (e.g., fifty dollars a week to rent a trailer shared with seven other men).[2] This creates a cycle of debt where the workers rarely see any money at all from their labors. All too often, farm owners manipulate the system to keep workers constantly indebted to them. These workers see none of their pay and are stuck at the job until they can repay their debt. Such situations have the potential to develop into forced labor and slavery schemes. The U.S. government has repeatedly uncovered slavery rings among farms in Florida, and in 2008, five farm owners were prosecuted for beating tomato harvesters, chaining them inside U-Haul trucks and forcing them to pick tomatoes against their will.[3]

Harmful working conditions are the norm. Safety standards are rarely met when workers spray fields with pesticides. Not only do such practices harm the local environment (and make their way into our produce), the workers' health is compromised by this intense, unprotected exposure to toxic chemicals. In addition, tomato pickers regularly face abuse, harassment, intimidation and (for female pickers) sexual harassment.[4] They endure all of this to work a job that earns them under two hundred dollars a week. Given the ubiquitous nature of the tomato in America, a lot of people are suffering to provide us with this commodity. As Senator Bernie Sanders (an independent from Vermont) commented in September 2008, "While slavery is, of course, the most extreme situation in the tomato fields, the truth is that the average worker there is being ruthlessly exploited. Tomato pickers perform backbreaking work, make very low wages, have no benefits and virtually no labor protections."[5]

In Florida, a local grassroots community group, the Coalition of Immokalee Workers, seeks everyday justice by opposing these practices and helping improve the lot of local tomato pickers. Their plea is that the farm managers stop taking advantage of their workers and respect their dignity instead. They initially succeeded in dismantling several slavery rings, and in 2001, they set out to raise the wages of tomato pickers. Their strategy involved a farm workers' boycott of the large fast-food chains (like Taco Bell, a major buyer of tomatoes), demanding that these chains take responsibility for the human-rights violations in the fields where their produce grows.

Numerous religious and human rights groups also supported the boycott, raising a collective voice on behalf of the tomato pickers. The campaign proved successful. In 2005 Taco Bell agreed to help raise wages by paying more for the tomatoes it buys. And in 2007, in a deal former President Jimmy Carter helped negotiate, McDonald's agreed to pay a penny more per pound to field hands who pick the restaurant chain's tomatoes.[6] As small as a penny-per-pound raise may sound, when workers are generally paid about forty cents per thirty-two-pound bucket, the extra penny would have nearly doubled their pay.[7]

Sadly these promised wages have not made it into the pockets of impoverished workers as the Florida Tomato Growers Exchange (FTGE) took legal steps to block any wage increase. They called the boycott and worker's coalition "un-American" and continue to insist that workers are already paid decent wages. The workers, church groups and anti-slavery organizations sent pleas to the FTGE asking them to stop opposing worker rights. As they await the outcome of that struggle, the workers and their supporters continue to put pressure on other large tomato purchasers to pay more for the tomatoes they buy.

The battle rages on as workers continue to suffer to bring us our unripe tomatoes. We can begin to see how this isn't just about eating a tomato; it involves an entire system that allows injustices against workers to flourish. In other words, God's creation and his image bearers are both harmed in the name of convenience and profit.

But God instructs his people to care for others through their farming practices or the farming practices they support. The Levitical law instructs farmers, "When you reap the harvest of your land, do not reap to the very edges of your field or gather the gleanings of your harvest. Do not go over your vineyard a second time or pick up the grapes that have fallen. Leave them for the poor and the foreigner" (Lev 19:9-10). The goal in God's economy isn't to maximize one's own profit but to make sure that a portion of one's crop went to those who needed it the most.

We read a story about this commandment in action in the book of Ruth. When Naomi and her daughter-in-law Ruth found themselves widowed and hungry after returning to Judah, Ruth (a foreigner in the land) helped them survived by gleaning what the harvesters left behind in Boaz's field. Boaz cared for the land and those in need in the way he farmed. This kind of practice requires a perspective of love and is a far cry from the Florida Tomato Growers' attempt to block the wage increases for impoverished migrant workers.

Cheeseburgers. If I have one weakness when it comes to food, it's cheeseburgers. Juicy meat smothered with rich cheddar cheese (and guacamole!) is hard to pass up. But besides being the iconic symbol of the backyard grill, the cheeseburger also has a story to tell that is far from pretty.

To increase dairy sales, the California Milk Advisory Board ran a series of nationwide ads commonly known as the Happy-Cow ads. These ads portray cows frolicking on fields of grass, living what appears to be the idyllic life. The implied message is that cows allowed to graze free in a relaxed environment are "happy cows," which therefore make better dairy products. While such free-range cows do make better dairy products (and may even be happy cows), these commercials don't come close to accurately portraying how Californian cows (or most cows) live.

Instead of idyllic existences on rolling, green hills, cows more often live on feedlots and factory farms. These high-capacity farms function more like a fast-paced assembly-line factory than the family farm of our cultural imagination. They cram thousands of cows into tightly packed pens or lots where they stand in their own muck and mire. Although cows are herbivores with a highly developed digestive system intended to digest grass, they are often forced to eat an unnatural diet of corn mixed with the ground-up remains of other animals and the refuse from poultry farms.[8] Such a diet fattens up cows quickly and produces meat and milk that is richer and higher in fat than what a grass-fed cow can make. To achieve maximum production results, owners often alternately force feed and starve cows with this unnatural diet. In addition many cows (in the United States) receive doses of hormones to increase milk production and growth.[9]

The result is a cheeseburger with some serious issues. Consuming an unnatural diet and hormones to increase milk production is not the way cows function best. Trying to digest such food causes cows to produce abnormally large amounts of methane gas. While the idea of cow farts might seem amusing in a junior high sort of way, it gets serious when we consider the sheer number of cows raised for our consumption today.

Methane is a greenhouse gas far more potent than carbon dioxide. An estimated 15 to 20 percent of methane gas emissions all over the world come from livestock. As the worldwide demand for meat continues to rise, the air pollution produced by cows increases as well. Agricultural areas in California are now some of the worst places in the country for air pollution. This pollution is not only harmful (and noxious) for those who live near a factory farm, but it is globally harmful as well. Livestock account for 18 percent of greenhouse gas emissions, generating more than all the cars, trucks and planes in the world.[10] These statistics have even prompted some to humorously point out that a Hummer-driving vegan (if such a thing exists) is technically more environmentally friendly than a Prius-driving meat-eater.[11] Many countries, including the United States, have even proposed "fart taxes" (as they have come to be known) on livestock to help offset the harmful emissions. But the real issue isn't that cows produce gas but that our demand for meat requires more cows than this world can sustain.

Groundwater pollution is also a problem. Much of the sixty-one million tons of waste produced by livestock each year in the United States makes its way directly back into the environment. In the crowded lots on the farms, the cows' excrement is left on the ground ready to be washed into groundwater, local streams and rivers with every rainfall. While we might think that it is natural for animal refuse to be part of the ecosystem, the concentration of waste from tons of cows in relatively small areas is a different story. The Environmental Protection Agency estimates that some thirty-five thousand miles of rivers and the groundwater in seventeen states are contaminated by factory-farm runoff.[12]

Besides the high quantity of excrement, the antibiotics regularly given to cows (to treat infections caused by their unnatural diet) also make their way into the environment and have serious consequences for other local wildlife. University of Illinois microbiologists documented that groundwater supplies are contaminated by antibiotic-laced-cow-waste, and this runoff contains drug-resistant bacteria. This bacteria flourishes and often kills other animals in the area, and can affect people as well. Fears of "superbacteria" (a drug-resistant bacteria that could lead to a deadly epidemic) aside, the runoff from these farms has real consequences for real people.

For Mark Thomas, an Iraq War veteran, and his family, this issue hit home. Soon after moving to the Pennsylvania countryside, they encountered pollution from a nearby hog farm that spreads its manure waste around local fields. The stench from the 450 hogs was nearly unbearable, but soon the family had to stop drinking their water as well. The pollutants in their water rose to nearly twice the federal health limit, and they kept getting sick with diarrhea and other digestive illnesses. Microbiologists linked this increase in illnesses to antibiotic-resistant bacteria caused by the antibiotics in the hog manure. Unfortunately, while the Thomas family tries to stay healthy and address the problem, the hog farm is expanding from 450 to 4,400 hogs. The hog farmers claim that spreading manure on fields is an age-old practice, but such high quantities of manure full of antibiotics are a very modern concern. The long-term consequences of such pollution remain to be seen, but the Thomas's are living with some of them right now.[13]

Besides concerns about pollution, factory farms present an issue when it comes to the efficient and sustainable use of resources.

Cows let out to pasture to eat a natural diet of grass feed off of the energy from the sun. Modern factory farms, on the other hand, bypass this natural energy source in favor of feeding the cows corn. This corn, purchased cheaply in the United States (thanks to government subsidies), requires vast amounts of fertilizers and pesticides. Combine those oil-based chemicals with the oil used to transport the feed, and we discover that feedlot cows are basically gas guzzlers, requiring between 250 to 300 gallons of gasoline to reach slaughter weight.[14] Similarly it takes an average 13 pounds of corn to produce 1 pound of meat, and it takes 792,000 gallons of water to raise a 1,000-pound steer.[15] In other words, a large amount of high-energy resources produce a very small amount of meat.

Feeding cows cheap corn (subsidized by our tax dollars) may lead to environmental destruction and waste resources, but it is the quickest, easiest and cheapest way to deliver beef to the demanding public. Fortunately, alternatives do exist that attempt to lessen these negative impacts. Organic free-range cattle, for instance, graze free on the grass God created them to consume. They don't receive antibiotics or hormones, and they generally live the "happy cow" life. These cows still have an impact on the environment (they use water and produce waste), but it is far less than those raised in the factory-farm system. However, you should assume that unless your meat or dairy is specifically labeled as "organic," "grass-fed" or "free-range" (not meaningless marketing terms like "natural" or "farm fresh"), it comes from a corn-fed, factory-farm cow.

LOVING OTHERS IN FOOD PRODUCTION

Of course, we must eat. Despite harmful production practices, giving up food is not an option. But we can take a faith-based and holistic view of the food we eat and the natural world that produces it. As author and farmer Wendell Berry writes,

This world, this Creation, belongs in a limited sense to us, for we may rightfully require certain things of it—the things necessary to keep us fully alive as the kind of creature we are—but we also belong to it, and it makes certain rightful claims on us: that we care properly for it, that we leave it undiminished not just to our children but to all the creatures who will live in it after us.[16]

While we might think that factory farms and chemical usage are modern inventions outside the scope of the Bible, we can still find guidelines in Scripture on caring for people and animals through our farming practices. In biblical cultures, farming was life. When a person's land and the animals are directly connected to their very survival, they are more likely to take care of them. This is the biblical concept of stewardship.

The concept of stewardship is easily misunderstood. Some people assume it means they have the right to dominate and destroy creation. Yet, when God told Adam and Eve to have dominion over the earth, he was not giving them license to exploit it but a command to care for it. For example, when we ask someone to house-sit for us, we expect them to watch over the house, feed our pets and generally take care of the place. We don't expect them to trash the house, destroy our cherished items and harm our pets. Similarly, God gives humans a responsibility to lovingly care for his creation, and he expects us to abide by his commands. To treat God's creation otherwise betrays the trust he places in us.

Wendell Berry refers to this trust when he writes that "our destruction of nature is not just bad stewardship, or stupid economics, or a betrayal of family responsibility; it is the most horrid blasphemy. It is flinging God's gifts into His face, as if they were of no worth beyond that assigned to them by our destruction of them."[17] To fail to care for the earth is to fail to care about God and care for our neighbor. Unfortunately, many of our modern farming practices do little to care for either, while some are actively doing harm.

In contrast to this, throughout the Bible we encounter the image of one who lovingly cares for his animals in the guise of a shepherd. From the young King David, to the beloved Psalm 23, to Jesus' parables, this image presents a beautiful portrayal of the protection, guidance and genuine care a loving shepherd provides. The Psalms express the belief that "The earth is the LORD's, and everything in it, / the world, and all who live in it" (Ps 24:1). The food we eat, the animals we raise and the land we cultivate all belong to God. They are not ours to be exploited or defiled; they are left in our care to be tended as a shepherd would his sheep. Destroying a community and causing diseases through our food-production practices doesn't live up to this biblical standard.

What we eat and how we produce it does matter to God. Food is more than just functionality or pleasure; it is part of the bigger picture of how we serve God. We eat every day, and if we are seeking to love God and love others every day, then our food choices matter. Eating becomes an ethical choice.

HOW TO EAT ETHICALLY

In considering how to eat ethically, I am drawn to the criteria proposed by J. Matthew Sleeth in his book *Serve God, Save the Planet*. He points out that while God doesn't give Christians in the New Testament specific dietary restrictions to follow (such as kosher laws), we shouldn't fail to apply the principles of Christian morality to what we eat. He identifies four in particular: First, in the case of a food shortage, people shouldn't eat more than their "fair share." Second, people should refrain from eating food obtained immorally—whether stolen, produced by child or slave labor, or from mistreated animals. Third, we should refrain from food that is harmful to us. And finally, we should refrain from "eating food if the growing, harvesting, storing, or cooking of it is harmful to others."[18]

Again, the phrase "you are what you eat" takes on new meaning in light of these moral considerations. In the food choices we make, we define our moral character. Choosing to support practices, even if by default, that exploit or harm others is a moral decision no matter how much we wish it were not. If workers in Florida live as slaves or receive substandard wages and abuse, we support those practices whenever we purchase the tomatoes they picked.

But let's be honest, sometimes it's a lot easier to simply not think about such things and to try to ignore the moral considerations

EVERYDAY PRACTITIONER

Josh Brown, graphic designer
Atlanta, Georgia

Until recently Josh typified the life of a suburban-church youth worker. He organized big event after big event and lived on a diet of endless pizza and fast food. But then he began to ask questions and started considering the holistic nature of faith. His questioning led him to realize that his whole life was a theological act. He came to believe that everything he did—how he ate, how he spent his money, how he spent his time—were all integrated with his faith.

What really struck Josh were the issues surrounding the food he ate. His fast-food habit reflected an industrialized food system that had little connection to historical and sustainable food-production practices. It disturbed him that his food choices, instead of being naturally connected to the earth, were actually harming creation. It bothered him as well that his desire for cheap food on demand often meant harmful consequences for the farmers who grow the food. In choosing to integrate his spirituality with his day-to-day choices, Josh realized that his choice to support the exploitation of Ecuadorian banana farmers (by buying and thereby demanding cheap bananas in December from companies that cheat their workers to turn a profit) said a lot about his perspective on God and the world. Such choices reflected his faith, so he decided to start making spiritually appropriate choices.

Josh didn't change everything overnight. He still ate fast food, but he started looking for ways he could care for the world and its inhabitants through his food choices. As part of this attempt, he started working a couple days a week at a local organic farm. In exchange for his work he received a share of the crops.

Josh soon discovered that growing food sustainably was hard work. Without coating the food (and the environment) with harmful pesticides and fertilizers, each weed had to be picked by hand. Food was no longer an abstract item that appeared at the grocery store, but it became a part of his life. In obtaining food this way Josh commented, "Your back aches. Your clothes are covered in dust and mud. There are no short cuts or easy ways. You smell everything. You feel everything. You see everything. You put every crop in by hand. And you take every crop out by hand." But the hard work pays off when he gets to eat the fruit of his labors and see how deeply connected he is to the earth.

Josh knows that people often complain that organic and locally grown food is too expensive, but his farming experience has helped him understand the true cost of such food. Sustainable food costs what it does because it isn't subsidized by government programs or the exploitation of people. To Josh the food he grows at the organic farm is "both entirely modest and extremely extravagant." The cost of his hard work and of altering his eating habits is worth the benefits of caring for the earth and loving God.[19]

Sleeth proposes when we go to the store. Truthfully, I myself don't always take the time to think about what I eat. As with many of these issues, I am still in the process of figuring out exactly how I need to alter my habits, without becoming a legalist or setting impossible standards. I still make food choices that cause harm to the earth and to others with my choices, but I am slowly working toward change. Without taking it slow, the enormity of the issue would lead me to throw up my hands in despair and do nothing at all.

It took a number of years after I first became aware of these issues before I even started making changes at all. I managed to tweak a few things in my life early on: I bought fair-trade coffee and joined the tomato pickers' boycott, but I did little else to change. The complexities of where to find ethical food and the questions of cost were the constant excuses I gave for not doing more. I realized, however, that eventually I'd have to take the plunge and make some more difficult changes.

Locavore: a person who supports environmentally friendly food production by choosing to purchase food grown in her local area.

So one year I decided to use the season of Lent to help me integrate ethical eating into my life. Lent is about sacrifice, but it is also a time of pursuing right relationships with God, with others and with ourselves—all of which are at the heart of seeking justice. So during that season I devoted myself to righting my relationship with others through the food I ate. I decided, as much as possible, to eat food that wasn't harmful to the environment, farmers or my body. This meant seeking out food that was fairly traded, organically grown and, often, locally grown as well (to support local farmers and reduce wasteful transport).

Lent that year proved to be one of the most meaningful I've ever experienced. To even find food to eat, I had to spend time re-searching stories about why our food choices matter. I had to come face to face with the struggles and injustices surrounding food, which forced me to reevaluate my own excuses. I stopped eating meat I knew harmed the environment and people, and I discov-ered sources for grass-fed, free-range beef. I bought a CSA sub-scription for my produce and in doing so supported a local farm-ing family. This family worked hard to protect the earth from toxic chemicals, they didn't exploit workers, they loved their animals, and they helped sustain a wide variety of heirloom produce (like the tomatoes mentioned earlier). My daughter enjoyed visiting their farm and playing with their goats, and I made friends with other families who chose to support this farm as well. Becoming deliberate about the food I ate helped me connect with both the land and with my community.

I'll admit that not every ounce of food that entered my mouth during that season met the ethical criteria, but I discovered that I was capable of doing a lot more than I had been. And unlike Lenten fasts that end come Easter Sunday, this discipline has stayed with me since that time. Quite honestly, there are many staples for which I can't yet find ethically sourced options, and I haven't fully abandoned them. Furthermore, as with chocolate, I don't reject the hospitality or company of friends. My family goes out to eat and also shares meals with friends, and in both places, I have no clue regarding the food's origins. Sometimes, even, life circum-stances have pushed me into easier and more "conventional" eat-ing habits (as when I was on pregnancy bed rest and my family subsisted on frozen tator tots and Chinese takeout). But it is a dis-cipline (and pleasure) my family continues to pursue as much as we are able.

One of the biggest objections regarding ethical eating, however, is that it costs too much. I often find that many people interested in eating this way simply don't think they can afford to do so. As

food costs rise around the world, choosing to eat ethically is often
not even considered because of higher price tags. The idea of ethical eating then gets resentfully labeled as a luxury for the rich. On
one level, the higher cost of ethical food is a reality. The sticker
price in the grocery store on an organic item is usually (but not
always) higher than a conventionally grown item. But that sticker
price never tells the whole story. Outside of the factory-farm system—with its safety hazards, its subsidies and its oppression of
workers—food does cost more. But the cost of food that is grown
sustainably without chemicals, and in ways that treat workers
fairly, simply reflects the full cost of the food we eat. Conventional
food ultimately costs the same (or more); it's just that the average
consumer isn't paying those costs himself in the checkout line.

Those costs, instead, get passed on to taxpayers or field workers or the environment (to be paid by our children). As Peter Singer
and Jim Mason write in *The Ethics of What We Eat,*

Organic food costs more partly because . . . intensive indus-
trial agriculture leaves others to pay the hidden costs of
cheap production—the neighbors who can no longer enjoy
being outside in their yard; the children who cannot safely
swim in the local streams; the farm workers who get ill from
the pesticides they apply; the confined animals denied all
semblance of a life that is normal and suitable for their species; the fish who die in the polluted streams and coastal
waters (and the people who previously caught and ate those
fish); and the unknown numbers of inhabitants of low-lying
lands in Bangladesh or Egypt who will be made homeless by
rising sea levels caused by global warming. It is understand-
able that people on low incomes should seek to stretch their
dollars by buying the lowest-priced food, but when we look
at the larger picture, the food produced by factory farming is
not really cheap at all.[20]

The choice becomes not just whether to buy "cheaper" food but deciding who will pay the cost of the food we buy. Will we assume the full cost or will we make someone with fewer resources pay part of the price for us? The issue is no longer just about saving a buck at the grocery store; it's about how we choose to treat other people.

That said, many Americans, for a variety of reasons, don't have the flexibility in their budgets to absorb the higher cost of sustainable and fairly produced food. I certainly don't expect those who have no idea where their next meal will come from to be able to make these choices. On the other hand, there are still plenty of Americans who manage to eat regularly even on a tight budget. For those of us in that category, there are steps we can take.

Rethink your eating habits: Cut out some meat. The best path to eating ethically isn't to simply switch to buying food with an organic label while maintaining the same level and pattern of consumption. Maybe, in order to eat ethically, we need to rethink our eating habits altogether. This can be hard for us, accustomed as we are to just walking into the grocery store and buying whatever we want when we want it. Many of us eat meat multiple times a day, buy out-of-season fruits and vegetables, and spend most of our grocery money on processed foods. Often just altering a few of those habits can make our eating habits more sustainable and more affordable.

Consider, for instance, the amount of meat we consume. Many Americans feel entitled to eat meat at least once a day. Asking them to restrict that consumption (even for their own health benefit) is typically met with extreme resistance (it might mean cutting back on my cheeseburgers!). The average American today eats around two hundred pounds of red meat, chicken and fish each year—an increase of twenty-three pounds from the 1970 average.[21] Increasing consumption is what raised the demand for cheaply produced options. As we saw earlier, though, these options have serious consequences. If our demand for cheap meat is fueling the proliferation of factory farms and all their ills, then reducing our consumption of meat is an easy way to reduce that demand. It's not necessary to go completely vegetarian (although that is a good option too, but I understand that it seems impossible for some to even consider) but to simply eat meat in moderation. If we eat less meat, we can then afford to purchase grass-fed beef or free-range chicken for the times we do eat meat. Reducing our consumption makes eating ethically easier to do.

Alter the foods you eat: Cook from scratch. A more involved step is to alter the sorts of foods we consume. Instead of opting for fast food or processed options, we can cook our food from scratch with whole, fresh ingredients. Besides being far healthier (and more loving toward our own bodies and our families'), and this may come as a surprise, cooking food from scratch, even with sustainably produced ingredients, is almost always cheaper than eating processed food. Making your own Spanish rice by cooking basic rice with spices costs less than a box of Spanish rice from the store (and generally has far less sodium and other chemicals). Baking your own whole-grain bread can cost less than a dollar a loaf and generally tastes even better than the $3.99 store-bought, organic variety. Making your own sun-dried (or oven-dried) tomatoes from what you grew in your own backyard or patio garden is insanely cheaper than buying them in a store. I've found that I can make a huge pot of organic butternut squash and carrot soup for less than the cost of a two-serving soup can of the same type. Or consider that the cost (and taste) of homemade pizza puts delivery options to shame.

Of course, I fully admit that it takes more time and effort to cook from scratch. I don't do it all the time, but I'm learning how to do it more. To do so, I had to personally commit to altering my schedule to make time for cooking food. I've had to learn how to actually cook things like homemade bread (my first few efforts weren't all that spectacular). Some days I really don't feel like putting in the effort and would much rather pop some frozen entrée in the microwave (and some days I do), but over time, I've learned how to save money and eat sustainably (not to mention healthier) by cooking very tasty meals mostly from scratch. I'm no frontier woman or iron chef, but this isn't an all-or-nothing issue. It's a process that I've had to work at but one that I've engaged at a comfortable pace.

CONCLUSION

Start simply. Choose not to eat meat one day. Cook a meal from scratch. Go to a farmers' market. Buy organic items. Do those things regularly. Then get more involved. Get to know the farmers at the market. Plant your own garden.[22] You could even do what I did and use the season of Lent to help you focus on making these changes. These are all small steps, but they add up. The next time you bite into a tomato or cheeseburger, think about what you are doing: is that action rooted in love, and if not, what changes can you make to ensure that it is?

FOR MORE INFORMATION

Books

Kingsolver, Barbara. *Animal, Vegetable, Miracle.* New York: HarperCollins, 2007. The beautifully told adventure of a family as they returned to living off the land for a year.

Singer, Peter, and Jim Mason. *The Ethics of What We Eat.* Emmaus, Penn.: Rodale, 2006. A detailed accounting of the ethical issues involved in our food choices.

Sleeth, J. Matthew. *Serve God, Save the Planet: A Christian Call to Action.* Grand Rapids: Zondervan, 2007. The story of how one family's Christian faith led them to alter their eating and lifestyle choices.

Movies

Fast Food Nation. Directed by Richard Linklater. 114 min., 20th Century Fox, 2006. A graphic drama that explores the horrors of factory farming, as well as the agricultural exploitation of workers.

Food Inc. Produced and directed by Robert Kenner. 93 min., Magnolia Pictures, 2008. A comprehensive overview of the injustices and dangers present in our highly industrialized modern food system.

King Corn. Written, produced and directed by Aaron Woolf. 90 min., DOCURAMA, 2007. An exploration of modern American farming and food consumption, which focuses on the main ingredient in our diet: corn.

Websites

Local Harvest
www.localharvest.org
A resource for discovering local farms and organic food sources in your area

The Meatrix
www.themeatrix.com
Award-winning series of short, animated films (modeled around the Matrix movies) that educate consumers about the factory farming system

The Coalition of Immokalee Workers
www.ciw-online.org
Follow the campaign for fair labor practices for agricultural workers

Faith in Place
www.faithinplace.org
An organization that helps faith communities become good stewards of the earth

Sustainable Table
www.sustainabletable.org
A great resource for discovering how to shop smart, eat well and support sustainable food

5

Clothes

THE STORY BEHIND WHAT WE WEAR

Kati smiled as she greeted Amanda. This was the perfect Saturday—nothing to do except wander around the mall, pretending they had enough money to buy everything that caught their eye. Homework could wait until tomorrow; today was all about having fun.

After stopping for smoothies in the food court, the girls made their way to their favorite clothing store: the "in" place for the latest fashions. Kati was glad Amanda was here; she always knew how to put together the best outfits—a skill Kati coveted.

Just inside the store, Kati held up an ultra-mini skirt and giggled. "My mom would *so* kill me if I ever wore anything like this."

"Well, it's not your color anyway," Amanda replied as she glanced over from the rack of shirts she was perusing. "But that totally reminds me. Do you remember that report Alex gave during current events in history the other day?"

"Do I ever remember anything from that class?" Kati replied, rolling her eyes.

"Seriously," Amanda laughed. "But the report was about this store. Something about overseas sweatshops where these women were like beaten for not making the skirts right or something."

"Oh yeah, I remember now," Kati replied as she moved to a different clothing rack. "Didn't Alex go off on some rant about human rights and how evil all that stuff was? Typical Alex. But I thought only places like Wal-Mart sold stuff made in sweatshops?"

"Who knows. It just popped into my head. How weird is that?" Amanda said as she selected a couple of shirts from the rack. "But, anyway, forget Alex and his rants, I'm going to go try these on. I so have nothing to wear to church tomorrow and need a new shirt to wear with that cute denim skirt I got last week. Did you find anything?"

"No," Kati sighed, aware of her nearly empty wallet.

"Oh well. That's okay. I'm sure Alex'll be happy you're not supporting sweatshops today," Amanda commented with a grin. Both girls laughed as they made their way to the dressing room.

☞

In the spring of 2007, I set out to purchase a new bra. But this shopping experience differed from my normal routine. Usually I would just hop in the car, drive to the nearest Victoria's Secret and buy some mass-produced, synthetic, hot pink thing that claimed to make me sexy. But this time I just couldn't do it. I had learned too much about how these garments were made, so I wanted to see if it was even possible to purchase an ethically made bra. So as my friends rolled their eyes and offered sarcastic "good lucks," I set my criteria and began my search for The Justice Bra.

First, the bra had to be made from an organically grown material. No synthetics made from petroleum, no pesticides that harm the environment and the farmers, and no unsustainable practices. These chemicals take a toll on the environment, as well as on human health, and I couldn't knowingly support that. So to be ethical, it had to be grown using ecologically friendly practices.

Second, it couldn't have toxic dyes in the fabric that hurt the environment and are potential carcinogens. I didn't want fish to die, or metals and chlorines to seep into my skin just so I could have hot pink.

Finally, the bra had to be fairly made. From the farmers who grew the fibers, to the weavers who spun the fabric, to the tailors who assembled it, each person along the way had to have received a living wage, not be coerced to work and treated humanely. Whoever made my bra needed to be able to make a living doing so. And not a degrading, oppressive living either, but one that respects her dignity as a human being.

Not too much to ask, I thought, *just an ethically made bra. I could find that somewhere, right?*

My quest didn't turn out to be easy. As I searched, I came face to face with two distinct worlds of justice issues: those who are passionate about caring for the environment, and those who seek justice for people. It appeared that ne'er the twain shall meet. I found sites where collective groups of women in Africa made clothing for fair wages, but they used cloth made with environmentally unfriendly practices. Or I found clay-dyed, organic cotton bras but had no clue about how they were made.

Finally, I found a commune in Canada that markets ethically produced bras. Made by various women's co-ops around the world, these organic, undyed bras were made under fair-labor guidelines. Mission accomplished.

But it bothered me that it was so difficult to find such an item. I wanted to spend my money in support of ethical practices, but finding clothing that fit the bill proved difficult. What, I wondered, is standing in the way of making ethical clothing easily accessible?

Clothing is a common part of life. We all need clothes, but

often the aspects of clothing we are most concerned with have nothing to do with where they actually came from. For example, The Learning Channel (TLC) airs a popular television show called *What Not to Wear*. On each show, two fashionistas descend on so-called fashion victims and force them to undergo a head-to-toe makeover—including purchasing a whole new (fashionable) wardrobe. The message is that there are certain clothes a person should not be wearing because they just don't look good or are a bit out of date. We live in a culture that devotes large amounts of time, energy and money to making sure we (and our clothes) look good. We think about what we wear, plan our outfits and shop for more to keep up with the latest styles. My purpose is not to discuss the validity of these behaviors, but merely to point out that, as a culture, we spend a lot of time thinking about the clothes we wear.

In all of our thinking about clothes, however, we often fail to consider the story behind the clothes we wear. By story, I don't mean what designer inspired one piece or another but the entire process of how that garment came into being. As with my search for The Justice Bra, there are all sorts of questions to consider when it comes to clothing: *What resources were used to produce the fabric? What chemicals were dumped into the environment to grow the fibers or to dye the colors? Who physically constructed the piece, and were they paid and treated fairly?* These questions are all part of the story of what we wear. In exploring these questions, I came to redefine my standards for "what not to wear."

Every day in the mail I seem to get some new clothing catalog, full of the latest fashions. And as a mother of small children who are constantly outgrowing clothes, shopping for clothes is a necessary part of my life. Yet the clothes I buy and wear don't just affect me; they are part of a global industry that affects all parts of the world. The garment industry employs some thirty to forty million people worldwide, and leaves its impact on their communities, environments, families and health.[1] It is easy to walk into a store and purchase whatever you think is cute and cheap enough for your budget. However, it is rare for the average shopper to stop and consider the hidden costs of what he is buying—and who might be paying those costs. So I want to highlight a few of those hidden costs and the impact they have on the people who make our clothes.

THE HIDDEN COSTS

It might be hard to imagine the environmental and health costs of our clothing because, since our clothes are not edible or mechanical, they seem generally benign and unassuming. Yet the process of creating the garment I am wearing impacts the world. Take the typical cotton T-shirt, for example. Printed in a rainbow of colors, with everything from school mascots to slogans (even environmental ones like "green is good"), these shirts have a long history. As I write this, I am wearing an AIDS awareness T-shirt I received as a freebie at a Christian ministry conference. A quick glance at the label told me it was made in Honduras for the Gildan label, and a quick Google search told me that that factory is under investigation for illegal working conditions.[2] Everything has a story.

The T-shirt's story begins in the cotton fields. These days, growing high-yield cotton uses large amounts of fertilizers and pesticides. Since cotton isn't intended for human consumption, there are few regulations regarding the amount of chemicals applied to this crop. Although cotton only uses around 3 percent of global agriculture land, it utilizes a quarter of the world's insecticides.[3] To keep up with the plummeting market prices for cotton, farmers use more and more chemicals in hopes of increasing production and thereby making more money.

For example, since the 1960s when development groups introduced foreign strains of cotton crops in India (along with new diseases and pests), the chemical-usage-rate increase resulted in the subsequent destruction of vast areas of land. As the pests and diseases developed immunity to the chemicals, farmers indiscriminately applied stronger and greater amounts with a "if a little is good, more must be better" mentality. As costs rose, soil and crop quality decreased, and while countries like the United States increased cotton subsidies (the economic benefits for farmers for simply growing cotton), India slashed theirs. A 2006 study revealed that many of these Indian farmers are actually taking their own lives (often by ingesting pesticides) because they are so in debt to the chemical suppliers and can no longer grow crops on ruined land.[4]

Most people assume that using these chemicals is a necessary part of modern agriculture, but their ubiquity often prevents us from recognizing their dangers. The pressure for high yields forces farmers to ignore future consequences. The struggle to live from harvest to harvest in a world economy out of their control is the farmers' main focus—not the costs to the environment or to human health (or future yield potential). To take just one example close to home, during the summer of 2008, I toured a Christian camp in the upper Midwest that can no longer use its main well due to the high concentrate of nitrates in the water. Cornfields surround the camp, and the pollution of the well stems from the fertilizers applied to those fields. The camp closed that well, but children around the world often have no such protection.

But, even as bad as the local environmental impact of chemical applications can be, the immediate effect on the agricultural worker is even more serious. In the United States, agricultural standards generally require workers to use respirators when they apply or are otherwise exposed to chemicals. Even still, the medical community reports between ten thousand to twenty thousand chemical poisonings among American agriculture workers each year.[5] U.S. government standards attempt to curtail these problems, but workers in many countries around the world don't have the benefit of this kind of protection and can rarely afford proper safety equipment, like the respirators needed for chemical use. The World Health Organization estimates that, worldwide, there are between two million and five million pesticide poisonings each year resulting in forty thousand fatalities.[6]

This unrestricted use of pesticides doesn't just affect the field workers either. Spraying pesticides on fields affects nearby children and can result in sickness and, occasionally, death. One such incident occurred in Benin in 1999. On that occasion, three boys between the ages of twelve and fourteen went to weed their father's cotton field when the field had just been sprayed with pesticide the day before. After they finished working, the boys ate some maize picked from an adjoining field. Within fifteen minutes, they started vomiting and were taken to a nearby hospital. The twelve-year-old died there from pesticide poisoning; the other two survived.[7] This family paid the high price of modern methods of growing cotton, and their story is all too familiar around the world.

Yet the impact of the chemicals used in making a T-shirt doesn't end with the harvesting of the crops. The process of dyeing and laundering garments carries its own hazards. In fact, all the basic clothing "innovations" we are accustomed to (wrinkle-free, flame retardant, UV blocking) require the use of chemicals on the fabrics. Many of the chemicals are highly toxic and are known carcinogens. In the United States there are strict standards for chemical usage and disposal, but as we saw before, such standards often don't exist in the developing world where most of our clothing is actually made.

The application and removal of such chemicals in the dyeing and laundering process result not only in chemicals in the clothing but also in the local wastewater. Many of these chemicals should be removed from the wastewater before it returns to the ecosystem, yet often the water remains untreated. The chemicals

saturate drinking water and fields of entire communities—
remaining in the environment for years to come—and they are
toxic enough to kill local wildlife. These communities often suffer
from high salt levels, toxicity and lack of oxygen in their water
supply as a result.

While the United States bans the most toxic and carcinogenic
chemicals, other countries still continue to use them in textile in-
dustries. Most of these are laundered out of the clothing before it
reaches the consumer, but it is impossible to remove all the chemicals. The more a piece of clothing "bleeds" when washed, the more
residual chemicals it contains that contact your skin and enter the
water system. But it is the workers who face the full brunt of exposure to these chemicals: cancer rates, infertility and menstrual dys-
functions are on the rise among workers in the textile industry.[8]
These are workers who typically get paid very little and have very
limited access to health care (not to mention their lack of means to
pay for such care). They are the ones who pay the price for the
quick and cheap production of large quantities of clothing to be
sold to consumers who expect variety at a low price.

It would cost the farmers and the textile factories more to abide
by safety standards, to use less toxic (but often more expensive)
chemicals or to develop less harmful procedures. In the world of
global competition, as companies seek to produce clothing as
cheaply as possible in order to turn a profit, the workers are the
ones who suffer. Yet this suffering isn't just limited to the health
and environmental impacts of exposure to chemicals; it often en-
compasses the entire working situation.

SWEATSHOPS

When media reports reveal the reality of clothing production,
consumers are usually horrified to discover the treatment of workers in sweatshop factories. Since 1996 when reports revealed that
twelve- and thirteen-year-olds in Honduras produced Kathie Lee

Gifford's clothing line for Wal-Mart, awareness of this issue has grown.[9] Every so often the media exposes a major label using sweatshops, prompting calls for higher working standards and a lingering suspicion among consumers regarding the clothing we wear. Yet, as the demand for cheap clothes remains high, sweatshops continue to thrive. Once again, it is the workers who pay the price for our savings.

These conditions aren't too hard to understand. Factory owners want to make a profit at what they do. Competition is fierce and clothing prices continue to drop as consumers demand cheaper and cheaper clothing options. This leaves factory owners with a choice: abide by standards and treat workers ethically and risk going out of business, or cut corners and try to save money wherever they can. Unfortunately, saving money usually comes at the expense of the workers. Basic workplace standards, like having a well-lit work area, getting breaks during the day, having proper safety equipment and getting paid at least minimum wage, can quickly turn into negotiable options in many factories (no matter what standards they officially abide by). The factory owners assume that to treat people fairly is to go out of business, so fairness and ethics are often left behind in the name of profit or simply economic survival.

SWEATSHOPS: working environments with dangerous conditions, where the workers have few rights and often work long hours for little to no pay.

Many clothing companies using textile factories have codes of conduct or "corporate social responsibility" contracts for the factories they use. Unfortunately, factory owners often ignore or subvert those guidelines. It is rare for clothing companies to inspect the factories that produce their clothes. They can send out guidelines, but factory owners, trying to make as much money as they

can and knowing they will not be held accountable, find it easy to
ignore them.

Sometimes it's hard to understand what all this means for the
workers. Hearing the stories of a few of the people involved in
making clothes for popular brands can help illustrate the problem. These stories made the news because the typical sweatshop
conditions eventually drifted into the realm of controversy, leading to exposure; other stories remain hidden without the attention
of the news media.

In 2006, reports came out that some two hundred to three
hundred children were found making garments for major U.S.
clothing companies, like Wal-Mart, Hanes and JCPenney, at a
factory in Bangladesh. These children were usually forced to
work fourteen-hour shifts and sometimes twenty-hour, all-night
shifts for around six cents an hour (rarely receiving pay for overtime hours). One thirteen-year-old girl described the effects of
the demanding schedule: "The long working hours make us feel
exhausted and very weak. When we return home after working
so many hours, we do not feel well, we are sick."[10] The children
reported beatings for failing to meet quotas or for making errors.
Supervisors restricted their bathroom usage, and they did not
have access to clean water. Those that passed out from exhaus-
tion were beaten and told to get back to work.

The children did not dare complain or tell their families about
the beatings, because they were all so desperate for money for
their families. Child labor is technically illegal in Bangladesh,
and the workers should be making closer to thirty-six cents an
hour. However, the children reported that, when outsiders came
by the factory, their supervisors hid them in the bathrooms.
They felt like they had no choice but to endure these conditions.
As one worker explained, the U.S.-bound clothing they make "is
made of the tears of children and the sweat of the workers."[11] The
factory owners exploited the children for profit. They were not

treated as real people but instead denied even the possibility of a childhood.

Workers rarely have the ability to speak out either. In 2007, a group of workers were arrested in Jordan for protesting the conditions in the factory they worked at. The factory employed them to make underwear for Victoria's Secret but had recently increased their hourly quotas to an impossible amount. They were guest workers in Jordan, who had personally paid nearly three thousand dollars for that job position and transportation there—often going into debt for the chance at a job. Legally, their employers promised them eight-hour workdays, a six-day working week, worker documents and a minimum wage of seventy-five cents an hour.

The workers soon found reality to be much different. They never received their documents, and so, unable to leave the factory grounds for fear of imprisonment by Jordan authorities, they were virtual prisoners at the factory. They generally put in fourteen- or fifteen-hour days, seven days a week, and overtime work was mandatory, although not always paid. The workers were short-changed an average of eighteen dollars a week—the equivalent of three days' wages. The dormitories where they lived had little access to water and were unheated, causing many of them to fall ill. Supervisors enforced daily quotas, and screamed at or beat workers who did not meet those quotas or who made a mistake. In November 2007, those quotas increased by 43 percent, placing impossible constraints on the workers. The few who chose to speak out against the new rules were arrested, imprisoned and beaten for a month, then forcibly deported.[12] Theirs is the real story and price of a pair of underwear.

Conditions like these exist in textile factories around the world. The employees are generally women and children who are often desperate for any job that brings in money for their families. For fear of losing their jobs, they endure the emotional and physical abuse. In some situations, women are raped and then forced by their supervisors to get abortions, with the implication that if they complain or refuse they will lose their job. Others accept wages that are far below the legal minimum (for their country), because, to them, something is better than nothing when even the official minimum wage is far below what the workers need to live on. Factory owners know how desperate the workers are, and they take advantage of that desperation. The result is a widespread system where people are used as mere tools and not respected as people. Their subjugation to humiliation, abuse and hazardous conditions represents our failure to love them and uphold their dignity.

THE BIBLE AND WORKER CONDITIONS

The Bible has much to say about the treatment of workers. God concerns himself with their well-being and cares whether they receive fair wages. Sweatshops that pay workers far below the minimum wage, or refuse to pay for overtime hours, are guilty of defrauding workers of their wages. These workers are counting on every cent they earn, but the emotional turmoil of never knowing what (or if) they will be paid adds to their daily stress.

Unfortunately, the temptation to treat one's workers unfairly and cheat them of their wages is a common practice today and was in the past as well. In Deuteronomy, the Israelites had to be instructed on how to respect workers:

> Do not take advantage of a hired worker who is poor and needy, whether that worker is an Israelite or is a foreigner residing in one of your towns. Pay them their wages each day before sunset, because they are poor and are counting on it. Otherwise they may cry to the LORD against you, and you will be guilty of sin. (Deut 24:14-15)

Making sure workers receive fair wages is just one aspect of how the Bible addresses worker conditions. Instructions are also given, in the Ten Commandments even, for ensuring that one does not overwork one's employees. Jesus reminds the Pharisees of these instructions on one of the many times they accuse him of breaking the sabbath. He points out to them that "the Sabbath was made for people, not people for the Sabbath" (Mk 2:27). While the Pharisees viewed the sabbath as a day of rules and legalism, it originally served to give workers a day of rest—to ensure they were treated rightly and not worked too hard. Consider the fourth commandment:

> Observe the Sabbath day by keeping it holy, as the LORD your God has commanded you. Six days you shall labor and do all your work, but the seventh day is a sabbath to the LORD your God. On it you shall not do any work, neither you, nor your son or daughter, nor your male or female servant, nor your ox, your donkey or any of your animals, nor any foreigner residing in your towns, *so that your male and female servants may rest, as you do.* Remember that you were slaves in Egypt and that the LORD your God brought you out of there with a mighty hand and an outstretched arm. Therefore the LORD your God has commanded you to observe the Sabbath day. (Deut 5:12-15, italics added)

While most of the other commandments are bare-boned instructions (don't steal, don't murder), this one comes with a reason. Observe the sabbath so that your servants may rest as you do. An entire day set aside to honor God and to treat people as people. A weekly reminder that all people bear God's image and deserve to be treated rightly. When the Pharisees seemingly forgot the intended purpose for the sabbath, Jesus not-so-subtly reminded them that the sabbath is for people—a reminder we need to hear today as well.

While many in the modern world no longer strictly observe the sabbath, we can still appreciate the spirit of this commandment. Ensuring that workers have time to rest and are not overworked is a concern of God's. He knows the hearts of people, that they will often sacrifice the dignity of others for the sake of profit. So God created a system that insisted on compassion and justice; he made caring for workers part of religious observance. There's no getting around it: treating one's workers well is part of what it means to love and obey God.

TAKING RESPONSIBILITY FOR WORKERS

It can be easy to distance ourselves from the issues surrounding clothing production. We care about others, but since we aren't causing the hardships directly, the plight of the workers falls into the out-of-sight, out-of-mind category. Often the major clothing companies see themselves in a similar light. They do not directly control the factories, so when sweatshop atrocities surface, they often disavow any wrongdoing and wash their hands of the matter. Instead of trying to improve conditions, they typically just cut ties with the factories, causing the workers to lose their jobs or face even harsher conditions as the owners scramble to make up for lost income. No one is willing to take responsibility for actually making things better, and again, the workers are the ones who ultimately suffer.

But the reality is that all of us who participate in the system have some responsibility for how it functions. Clothing companies should be responsible for how their clothes are made. They should insist on healthy and environmentally friendly production. They should inspect the factories and ensure that they adhere to the codes of conduct. They should ask what pushes factory owners to cheat workers of wages (are the owners not getting paid a decent price for the clothing to begin with?). Instead of abandoning sweatshops when they are revealed by the media, companies should instigate reforms and make recompense to the hurt and cheated workers. Seeking justice in these ways involves not just admitting guilt but also requires taking responsibility by helping restore the dignity of those they have, perhaps inadvertently, wronged. True justice always involves healing and restoration of the broken.

But we shouldn't just point fingers at the big clothing companies. As consumers we too share responsibility for the clothing we buy. If we purchase items made by underpaid and abused workers, we participate in their exploitation. Acknowledging our role in the system, and that we are the ones affecting the demand for cheap clothing, is the first step in changing how the entire system works. In the Western world we take full closets and the ability to purchase lots of clothing at cheap prices for granted, but sadly, we often don't consider the human cost of that lifestyle. I doubt most of us want people to be cheated or exposed to toxic chemicals or abused just so that we can have lots of clothing. And while we may acknowledge that those things are disrespectful and even evil, the real question is whether we will allow such convictions to affect our shopping habits. Seeking justice involves choosing to live rightly in respect to all people. Are we willing to make the changes needed in our habits to help change the system?

As with coffee and chocolate, alternative clothing options exist. As I discovered in my search for The Justice Bra, although these options are still developing, it *is* possible to find clothes produced in ways that ensure the dignity, health and well-being of the worker. These alternatives allow consumers to opt out of the traditional system and communicate with their pocketbooks for how they want workers to be treated. These options include clothing made under fair-trade standards, clothing that is guaranteed to be sweatshop free or clothing that is made with organically grown fibers that have not been treated with harsh chemicals. Since my quest in 2007, I've discovered numerous online stores and even some major brand names that carry clothing options in a variety of styles that meet these standards. Seeking out ethically made clothing no longer has to be an ordeal.

Choosing ethically made clothing is part of what is necessary to assume our responsibility in treating workers well. Instead of shoring up a corrupt system by giving money to companies that exploit their workers, we can support companies that care for their workers and ensure that they get a fair wage for their labors. Generally, ethically made clothing will display whether it is made from organically grown fibers and will display a fair-trade or sweatshop-free label. It is usually easy to spot the label on clothing produced in these ways, because manufacturers want you to know when they are making an effort to be ethical.

Excuse #1: Ethically made clothing isn't stylish. As simple as just purchasing ethically made clothing sounds, there are a few issues that often stand in people's way. The first is the assumption that ethically made clothing isn't stylish. While part of me questions the need to place style above loving others, I understand that this is a big deal for a lot of people. The stereotype of organic or fairly made clothing is that it is intended for "hippies"—you know, long flowing skirts, lots of rough-woven hemp, tribal patterns. While such clothing does exist (and can be found in my closet), it is far from being the only ethical option out there. Fairly made clothing exists that is just as trendy and "normal" as anything you can find in a traditional store. It may be harder to tell that it is alternative clothing since it looks just like what everyone else is wearing, but you will know what you are supporting with your purchase.

Excuse #2: Ethically made clothing is more expensive. The second issue that often arises when purchasing ethically made clothing is the price. If you are accustomed to buying really cheap clothing from the typical big-box store, the cost of ethical clothing will seem high. I can relate to the desire to shop frugally, but to overcome this hurdle, it may be necessary to step back and consider the hidden costs of the eight-dollar shirt we might typically buy. For a shirt to cost that little, usually the workers who made it had to be paid very little as well. While the reverse is not also true—that because something costs more, the workers must have received a fair wage—it is true that if a worker receives a fair wage (and better working conditions), the cost of an item *will* be more. Most ethical clothing companies are bringing in less profit than conventional ones even though the price tag on their clothing may be higher. The question boils down to whether we are willing to pay a price for our clothing that ensures that workers were treated well. Often that price isn't that much more than conventional prices, but it can still be a difficult choice to make.

Speaking personally, I do my best to seek out ethically made items when I need a new item of clothing. This means that I spend more on each item, but to compensate, I simply buy fewer clothes. It has forced me to realize how often I buy clothing just because I want something new. Being deliberate about my shopping helps me put those habits in perspective, revealing to me my needs versus wants, and this actually saves me money.

To be perfectly honest, though, I still struggle with purchasing ethical clothing for my children. For kids who need a whole new wardrobe a couple times a year, I honestly cannot afford the ethical price tag. I tend to buy a few items and wish I could do more. But I also try to seek out alternative ways to avoid supporting the conventional system, like borrowing from friends or shopping at garage sales and resale shops. I understand how much of a struggle this issue can be. I understand that many people don't have the means to buy new clothing at all. Yet I've also observed that no matter what a person's income, new clothing often becomes a priority in our fashion-obsessed culture. Rethinking that priority and reevaluating what you buy is part of what it means to seek justice in this area. This is more than just a price-tag issue, and there are ways to make it work, even if that requires altering habits or making sacrifices.

Excuse #3: I can't find clothing that is ethically made (in all areas). The third major issue is discovering which items are ethically made and where you can find them. As in my search for The Justice Bra, I often encounter sites that sell clothing made, for example, by a women's co-op that ensures good working conditions and fair pay, but the site gives me no information about the environmental or health impact of the fabric production. Similarly I can find organic cotton clothing but with no information regarding worker conditions. The most frustrating is when I find an item for sale that was neither produced in environmentally friendly ways, nor made under fair-labor standards, but which will donate 1 percent of its profits to some charity cause. This helps the buyers feel good about their purchase but distracts from the underlying justice issue. What we need, instead, is for public awareness of these issues to increase and for the demand for clothing made ethically (in all aspects) to increase. As demand increases, more clothing companies will be forced to take responsibility for the clothing they sell.

One group committed to raising awareness about ethically made clothing is the Bold Women of the Netherlands.[13] Members of this group help spread information about where people can find socially responsible stores, but they also encourage retailers to start carrying ethically produced items. They aren't timid in their encouragement either, often participating in over-the-top publicity stunts that can't fail to capture attention. Members created what they call the Buyer's Army—a group of women who march on department stores, dressed in army fatigues with hot pink accessories. Their goal is to fill their shopping baskets (hot pink, of course) with ethically produced items from that store. Often such items cannot be found, but they have no qualms about asking salespeople the hard questions regarding the items in the store: "How can you be sure this cushion wasn't made by children?" and "What percentage of the sales price of the chocolate bar goes to the cocoa farmer?" These questions are uncomfortable, but they raise awareness about what it means to be an ethical consumer.

Being willing to ask those questions of ourselves, the clothing companies and the retailers can help increase the availability of such items and start improving the conditions of global workers. The Bold Women of the Netherlands have fun raising awareness. We can be as creative as they were. Or we can stick to more conventional methods—sending letters to the brands you like and the stores you shop at is a simple way to let those companies know that you are a customer who cares about the ethical treatment of workers, and you are willing to pay a fair price for what you buy. College students across the nation are even pushing to make their campuses "sweat free." They believe workers shouldn't be oppressed to make a T-shirt with the school logo on it for them.[14] Slowly but surely the message is getting out as everyday people commit to seeking justice in whatever ways they can.

Beyond choosing to shop more ethically, another way to address this issue is to carefully consider how we can challenge the system of exploitative labor by reducing the amounts we consume. We must ask ourselves how much we really need and adjust our desires to fit better with what the world can reasonably and ethically meet. So while seeking to buy organic, fairly made clothing is a good thing, it should also be balanced with one's needs. I honestly have very few ethically produced items in my closet. I've bought them as the need has arisen and received a few things as gifts, but I didn't throw out all of my old clothes and go shopping for a whole new (ethical) wardrobe. I also don't turn down clothing gifts from friends or family, and I have had difficulty finding ethical options for certain sorts of items. For me this isn't about legalistic shopping; it's about pursuing a new direction as best I can, whenever I can.

Excuse #4: If I don't buy ethically made clothing, at least the workers in sweatshops will still have jobs. Of course the economics at play here are complicated. Our global system both employs and harms workers. Some might say it would just be better for me to buy as much as I can to keep workers employed. They question the call for factories to treat workers fairly, claiming that will put other workers who are desperate for jobs out of work. Such arguments claim that workers are grateful for their jobs in sweatshops, because those jobs are better than nothing and to stop sweatshops will destroy their lives.

I am disturbed by the assumption that a worker's only options are a horribly abusive job or no job at all. Such a view assumes reform is impossible and that conditions can never improve. The call to eliminate sweatshops is not a call to shut down factories (which is too often the path taken by clothing companies caught in unethical behavior); it is a call to improve conditions in those factories. The point is not to destroy jobs and lives but to bring healing to those already broken.

For example, in 1996 news leaked out that Disney used sweatshops in Haiti to produce some of its clothing.[15] The conditions in these factories involved long work hours, beatings and pay far below a living wage. Workers as young as ten stitched Aladdin T-shirts there. Other workers had recently been hospitalized due to toxic-fume exposure. Since Disney represents the innocence of childhood to many Americans, the public outcry was extreme. Outraged consumers called for Disney to take responsibility for their actions and improve conditions. Instead Disney's response was to shut down the factory in Haiti and move it to China where they could pay workers even less.

Around the same time, the sweatshop conditions in certain Nike factories in China publicly surfaced. Instead of running from the problem, Nike committed to reforming its factories and ensuring its codes of conduct are followed. Things aren't perfect in their factories, and as of 2008, violations and problems continue to be reported, but Nike continues to work hard to make changes.[16] The well-being of their workers wasn't just an issue of a one-time scandal but an ongoing goal to be achieved.

CONCLUSION

Responses like Disney's must be avoided, and responsible leadership like Nike's must be encouraged. Raising awareness should not lead companies to abandon people and seek to hide their sins but should lead to genuine reform. These companies need to know that we, their customers, want them to be global good citizens. We don't control their boardrooms, but we are the ones buying their products. Continuing to hold them and ourselves responsible is the everyday justice we can seek.

Awareness about the production conditions of our clothes, and love for those who make them, cannot remain in the realm of ideals; it must translate into action. We can choose to buy clothes made under decent and fair conditions, send messages to companies, and alter our consumption habits. Clothing companies will see no need to start treating their workers well unless consumers send that threefold message. Seeking everyday justice for workers starts with these small changes in each of our lives. But small changes add up and can eventually change the whole system. So next time you ponder "what not to wear," remember that how you answer has global implications with very personal meaning for individual workers.

FOR MORE INFORMATION

Books

Hartman, Laura P., Denis G. Arnold and Richard E. Wokutch, eds. *Rising Above Sweatshops: Innovative Approaches to Global Labor Challenges.* Westport, Conn.: Praeger Publishers, 2003. A variety of perspectives on how to end our dependence on sweatshop labor.

Rosen, Ellen Israel. *Making Sweatshops: The Globalization of the U.S. Apparel Industry.* Berkeley: University of California Press, 2002. A very in-depth look at trade policy, the rise of modern sweatshops and the worldwide dangers they represent.

Ross, Robert J. S. *Slaves to Fashion: Poverty and Abuse in the New Sweatshops.* Ann Arbor: University of Michigan Press, 2004. This book explores the history of modern sweatshops, the policies that keep them in place, the ethical issues they pose and a variety of approaches to ending the need for them.

Snyder, Rachel Louise. *Fugitive Denim: A Moving Story of People and Pants in the Borderless World of Global Trade.* New York: W. W. Norton, 2008. A detailed look at the hardships and horrors of making and selling blue jeans.

Movies

China Blue. Directed and produced by Micha Peled. 87 min., Teddy Bear Films, 2005. A clandestine look at the hardships faced by young girls working in a Chinese blue jean factory.

The Corporation. Directed by Mark Acbar and Jennifer Abbott. 145 min., Zeitgeist Films, 2005. An exhaustive look at the modern-day corporation that pursues profit and power above all else.

Wal-Mart: The High Cost of Low Price. Directed and produced by Robert Greenwald. 98 min., Brave New Films, 2005. A contrast of the public image Wal-Mart presents, and the human and environmental toll of its actual practices.

What Would Jesus Buy? Directed by Rob VanAlkemade. 91 min., Arts Alliance America, 2007. A sobering look at America's addiction to shopping.

Websites (including shopping resources)

Behind the Label
www.behindthelabel.org
Current news about sweatshops

The National Labor Committee
www.nlcnet.org
Putting a human face on our global economy

New American Dream Conscious Consumer Guide
www.newdream.org/consumer/clothing.php
Information regarding the labor practices of companies and shopping alternatives

Clothing Resources (just a sampling representing a variety of styles and prices)

Be the Change Elements
www.btcelements.com

Ecoland
www.ecolandinc.com

Fair Indigo
www.fairindigo.com

Indigenous Designs
www.indigenousdesigns.com

No Sweat Apparel
www.nosweatapparel.com

Rawganique
www.rawganique.com

Simple Shoes
www.simpleshoes.com

Taraluna
www.taraluna.com

Tinctoria Designs
www.tinctoriadesigns.com

Waste

THE HIGH PRICE OF OUR DIRTY LITTLE HABITS

Maria pulled into the Costco parking lot, grateful that her mom was picking up the kids from daycare so she could run a few errands. She'd learned the hard way that taking young children into that maze of free samples was a sure way to spoil their dinner. She grabbed the shopping list she'd quickly jotted down over her lunch break earlier and headed inside for some uninterrupted shopping.

Being an efficient person, Maria appreciated the opportunity to buy in bulk and keep her large pantry well stocked. Her life was too busy already to have to deal with something as annoying as running out of toilet paper, so she always stayed prepared by making regular trips to the discount warehouse.

Although tempted to browse through the table of books, Maria immediately started on her shopping list. Toilet paper and paper towels, of course. Diapers, Pull-Ups® and wipes for the little one. Tampons and sanitary pads for her. Sandwich bags and plastic utensils for the older kids' lunches. Paper cups and plates for the party this weekend. And a couple cases of bottled water for her to take to work. Check, check and . . . check.

Maria maneuvered her burgeoning cart to the checkout and struggled to unload the oversized boxes. She watched wistfully as the total of her items climbed higher and higher. As much as she loved buying in bulk, it was always a shock to the bank account.

As she walked back out to her car and started attempting to fit everything into her trunk, Maria considered her receipt. Spending $225 on supplies was never a welcome occurrence, but as she wedged the box of diapers in the tight space left and closed her trunk, she was suddenly struck by the strange thought that she had just spent over $200 on, essentially, *trash*. Money was tight and it just felt wrong to know that she spent so much on items she would soon be throwing away.

As she drove out of the parking lot, Maria sighed. She wondered if there was an alternative to such a "throwaway" lifestyle, but she knew her life was just too busy to think about that right now. She would have to continue to pay the price for efficiency and ease.

☞

In a 1997 yacht race from California to Hawaii, Captain Charles Moore decided to attempt a shortcut through a seldom-sailed area of the Pacific Ocean. Expecting to merely face the odd currents common to that area, Moore discovered instead a vast sea of trash.[1] Captured by the swirling currents, this "plastic soup" stretched for thousands of miles and contained an endless number of plastic bags, discarded toys, syringes, lighters and other debris too durable to biodegrade. Washed-away beach debris, accidental shipping mishaps and deliberate dumping into the ocean all end up in this dead space, carried and then trapped there by the never-ending currents.

After this experience, Moore (ironically, an heir to an oil fortune) sold his business interests and committed his life to environmental activism. This "Great Pacific Garbage Patch" is already twice the size of the continental United States, and it continues to grow. Sea life is trapped and killed in its clutches, and toxic chemicals collect in the absorbent plastic, ultimately entering our food supply.[2] Yet, as Moore warns, unless we seriously reduce the amount of waste we produce, the problems will only increase.

We live in a disposable society. If it breaks we don't fix it, we replace it. If it is out of date, we upgrade. If it may require cleaning, we opt for alternatives we can just throw away. Our society is structured around this mindset. It is cheaper to us, in the moment, to replace than to repair. Our cell phones, computers and cars seem programmed to fall apart just past the warranty date. Our clothes lose their shape, color and stitching after a handful of washings. And our solution is to throw it all away.

For many in the world, this disposable lifestyle is a symbol of wealth—a person can afford new items and the status they convey. Since their introduction into mainstream society, disposable items were promoted as a means to help people feel rich, granting them the ease and cleanliness usually only available to those with money for servants. The twin lures of status and convenience proved too tempting to resist, so over the last century, we have slowly become a disposable society. Product by product, we have accepted the advertised promises of modernity, ease and better lives—without much regard for long-term costs. We buy, we throw away, and we buy some more. Our ability to consume is matched only by our ability to dispose.

The United States produces more trash per capita than any other nation in the world, with the average American producing four-and-a-half pounds of trash per day.[3] Items that our ancestors would have patched, reused or creatively recycled, we toss into the garbage can with little thought and almost no regret. Regarding this shift in attitude toward our waste habits, writer Elizabeth Royte notes, "it is easier to discard a ready-made dress, cut and stitched in an unknown sweatshop . . . than it is to throw away something you or your mother made."[4]

I remember reading the Little House books by Laura Ingalls Wilder as a child. I recall wondering why Laura only had two dresses: an everyday dress and a Sunday dress (both were hand-me-downs from her older sister). I didn't have a ton of clothes (and much of what I did have was, in fact, a hand-me-down or something hand-stitched), but I had far more than just two dresses. In the past century, our lives have changed. We now own more clothes, more labor-saving devices and more entertainment items than our predecessors would ever have dreamed possible. Some may see such acquisition as a sign of progress, but "progress" always comes at a price.

As a culture we have grown increasingly wasteful in our materialism, stripping the land of its resources at an alarming rate, and dumping our waste into the environment with reckless abandon. Instead of being faithful stewards of this earth, we exploit and use it for our own selfish ends. I know I'm part of the problem; disposable habits are hard to break. And this is a problem that has no easy solutions. We can alter lifestyles and shopping habits, but for sustainable and relevant change to occur, we need to shift our entire perspective.

The biggest shift that needs to take place is to remember that the earth belongs to God and that he expects us to be good stewards of it—not only for the sake of the creation but for our own sake as well. This world is our home, and a redeemed version of it will continue to be our home for eternity after the resurrection of the dead. Yet instead of lovingly taking care of our home, we have, literally, trashed the place.

While the oceans of floating garbage, as well as the mounds of trash you can find lining the streets in slums around the world, are disgusting and provoke revulsion, the issues go much deeper than "sight pollution." Landfills to hold our waste not only take up land—a limited resource in our world—they also release toxic chemicals into our environment. The EPA estimates that 75 percent of landfills in the United States are currently leaking.[5] These leaks leach whatever is in the landfill into the surrounding environment, often causing irreversible damage to groundwater supplies. The byproducts of our disposable lifestyle also lead to chemicals like PCBs, lead, solvents, dioxins, DDT, benzene, CFCs and furans seeping into the surrounding land and water, which then leads to the release of methane, carbon dioxide, vinyl chloride and hydrogen sulphide into the air.[6] Many of these are toxic chemicals, poisonous to people and devastating to local ecosystems. And that's just the items "safely" disposed of in approved landfills. Other items are dumped directly into rivers and oceans, causing immediate pollution. Obviously, the waste crisis is huge and is affecting our world in serious ways.

A BRIEF LOOK AT EVERYDAY ITEMS

I want to set the stage by examining the impact on the world around us of a few common waste items. These items represent and signify trends in our culture and our attitudes, but they are certainly not the sum of the problems. Eliminating these items won't suddenly make the world all better or put an end to the environmental damage of waste. They are just examples, but significant nonetheless, and I hope they can help us rethink how we consume and dispose of this world's resources.

Electronics. Our society is wired. Electronics are such a common part of everyday life that it is hard for those of us under forty to even recall a time when things were different. I sit here writing this on a laptop that is wirelessly connected to the Internet while my husband works on his laptop across the room. My cell phone sits beside me, and the sound of medieval chants by Catholic monks plays from my iPod nearby. I am surrounded by technological equipment I didn't even own three years ago.

While helping my mother make travel arrangements online recently, we discussed how we couldn't even remember how we did such things before the ease of the Internet. Electronics are just a part of who I am these days. I like technology and would have a very hard time disconnecting myself from that world, but within a society obsessed with new and rapidly changing gadgets, I've come to see that I must indulge in my electronic habits responsibly.

Simply put, the electronics our society consumes (and disposes of) at a rapidly increasing rate are toxic. Filled with heavy metals (like lead, mercury and zinc), the EPA deems most electronic waste hazardous and mandates its proper disposal (at electronics- or hazardous-waste centers). But the average consumer either doesn't know that rule, or chooses not to follow it, because our landfills are quickly filling up with more and more electronic waste. Some estimate that approximately 150 million personal computers currently sit in landfills, a number projected to rise dramatically over the next few years.[7] Electronic waste is the single largest source (40 percent) of lead in landfills, which is no huge surprise, given that the average computer monitor contains four pounds of lead.[8] These are hazardous materials that eventually enter groundwater supplies and contaminate the environment.

Finding solutions and alternatives for electronic waste isn't easy. In many communities, discovering how and where to dispose of items takes time and research. Hazardous waste sites often close or stop accepting certain forms of waste. Consumers must often choose between paying large sums of money to properly dispose of an item (once they finally figure out how) or just slipping it in with the rest of the landfill-bound trash.

I recently attempted to recycle a couple of old cell phones at a store that claimed to recycle these items. Contrary to their advertisements, they didn't recycle phones directly but instead gave me a website where I could find out where to mail the phones. What I thought would be a simple act turned into a multiday process of researching, driving around and spending money. I knew I didn't want to dump the phones into our ecosystem, but I wonder how many people are willing to put up with the hassle of proper disposal.

These kinds of hassles prompt some to demand that electronics manufacturers take responsibility for the proper disposal of the products they produce. This, in part, addresses the issue of "planned obsolescence" in electronics, but these days, planned obsolescence, although annoying, is generally accepted as a fact of life. However, back in the 1950s these same practices sparked huge debates (e.g., is it ethical to build into an item its own self-destruction, merely for the sake of acquiring greater profits?). Some believe we should revive those debates today for the sake of the environment. They believe corporations should take care to build longer-lasting products, which would reduce the amount of electronic waste over time.

PLANNED OBSOLESCENCE: the deliberate engineering of products to break after a given amount of time, requiring consumers to spend more money to replace the product.

Others are more cynical about the likelihood that any corporation would willingly sacrifice profits for the sake of the environment, so these people seek to at least hold them responsible for disposing of their products once they become waste. Some states are working on legislation that would require electronics companies to be responsible for the recovery and recycling of electronic waste. Such laws are already present in many European countries, with the cost of disposal already built into the initial price of the items. This forces both the producer and the consumer to think long-term and be aware of the impact of any purchase.

Some companies are already jumping onboard with electronics collection and recycling. Stores like Costco have trade-in programs where you can actually get money back for certain electronics (others are simply recycled). Other stores like IKEA help make shoppers aware of the end result of their waste habits by not only providing recycling opportunities but also labeling their trash cans with the term "landfill."

Theoretically, recycling electronic waste should be a money saver for corporations. Reusing heavy metals like lead is far easier and cheaper than mining them. But the infrastructure for safe recycling isn't widespread in the United States, and the government generally subsidizes virgin-mining operations. Until structures are in place and systems change, these expensive and precious, yet toxic, metals will continue to be thrown away—or else sold overseas to countries eager for easy and cheap access to expensive metals.

Nearly 80 percent of electronic waste that is recycled in the United States ends up being sold overseas.[9] While the idea of recycling this metal is good on one level (it's better environmentally than strip mining or dumping things in landfills), problems arise because of the lack of environmental laws in many of those countries. As electronic waste gets recycled (smelted down) in these countries, the toxic byproducts of that process spread into the surrounding environment. In La Oroya, Peru, for example, a group of farmers recently brought charges against a local lead, zinc and copper smelting plant for contaminating their fields and rendering them useless. Investigations of the area in 1999 by local health officials also discovered that 99 percent of the children there suffered from lead poisoning.[10]

To discover how to recycle electronic waste (and just about anything else) in your area, visit Earth911.com

I don't think any of us expect to contribute to the destruction of children's health when we drop off our computers at a local recycling center. Choosing to protect our groundwater shouldn't mean that we have to participate in the destruction of the soil, water and air of another community. Many of us want better options. At this point I still choose to recycle and also seek out ways to increase corporate responsibility and safe recycling options, but I am also rethinking my lifestyle and the waste I produce as a consumer. I'll come back to that option, but first I want to take a look at another common source of waste in our society.

Diapers and sanitary pads. Yes, that's right . . . diapers and sanitary pads. At this point male readers of this book might be tempted to skip ahead to the next section and ignore the icky "women's" problems. However, I encourage you to fight that urge and, instead, partner with women to help find workable solutions to reducing waste in these areas. Sanitary pads are obviously female-specific, but most men live in a household with women who currently use them (or will someday use them). And being educated can never hurt! As for diapers, everybody knows that real men change diapers, so there are no excuses on that account (yes, my husband does most of the diaper changing in our house). And if, for some reason, your existence never brings you into contact with women or children, here's an introduction to an entirely new world.

In this disposable age, fewer things have captured our fascination with the ease and convenience of one-time use than those that deal with bodily refuse. A majority of us embrace the concept of capturing this waste in a paper/cotton/plastic device, wrapping it in more paper or plastic, and throwing it away—never to be thought of again. Unless our town threatens to build a landfill in our backyard, most of us never think twice about this system. The disposable lifestyle is so ingrained in our culture that the term "disposable diaper" seems redundant, and the mere suggestion of reusable alternatives is generally met with disgust and ridicule. But this out-of-sight, out-of-mind attitude has had serious effects on the environment as the numbers of disposables add up.

Diapers are the third largest source of waste in landfills today. The typical American baby uses between six thousand and ten thousand diapers before learning to use the toilet (which, thanks to the high efficiency of "no-wetness" diapers, is occurring at later and later ages). This means around 18 billion diapers are dumped into landfills each year—single-use items that took 82,000 tons of plastic and 1.3 million tons of wood pulp to produce.[11] The numbers are similar when it comes to sanitary products. In her lifetime, the average American woman will use around sixteen thousand tampons (and applicators) and about twice as many sanitary pads. This usage results in roughly 6.5 billion tampons and 13.5 billion sanitary pads (plus packaging) disposed of each year. The numbers are staggering and betray our addiction to waste, but they don't even begin to reveal the full environmental impact of these choices.

Diapers and sanitary products have an environmental footprint long before they enter our homes. Consider the raw materials needed to produce these single-use items. Each diaper requires about a cup of crude oil to produce. In our world of dwindling oil supplies (and rising prices), I wonder if disposable products are really the most efficient use of that oil. Further, the cotton used in these items generally uses vast amounts of pesticides to grow conventionally, and harsh chemicals are used in the production of the final product, chemicals that are both released into the environment and come in contact with the most intimate places on our bodies.

One such chemical used is chlorine. Since our culture regards the color white as clean and sterile, companies use chlorine gas to bleach diapers and sanitary products, giving us the illusion of sterility. However, as a byproduct, this process also produces the toxic chemical dioxin, which causes cancer, birth defects, liver damage and skin diseases. The EPA lists dioxin as the most toxic chemical linked to cancer.[12]

Also present in the powder used in diapers to make them super-absorbent is sodium polyacrylate (the gel stuff you see if the diaper bursts open). In 1985, authorities banned a similar form of this chemical from being used in tampons, because of its connection to toxic shock syndrome.[13] Yet despite being lethal if ingested—and being reported to cause severe skin irritations, oozing blood from perineal and scrotal tissues, fever, vomiting, staph infections in babies, and even hemorrhaging, cardiovascular failure and death in lab rats—it is still commonly used in diapers. These and other chemicals in diapers also have links to male infertility. While the diaper companies dispute the validity of these findings, I find myself amazed, not only at our willingness to dump these chemicals into our environment during the production and disposal of diapers and sanitary products, but also at our willingness to expose our bodies and our babies to them day after day.

The most common concern with diapers and sanitary products, however, is the effect that dumping so much human waste straight into landfills has had and will have on the environment. The diaper itself will take over five hundred years to decompose, but the issue of untreated human waste introduced directly into the ecosystem is a cause of immediate concern. Of course, it is technically illegal to dump human waste in a landfill. If you read the fine print on most diaper packages, the instructions are to dump the waste in the toilet and rinse the diaper before disposal. *Seriously.* Take a look the next time you are at a store. I don't know about you, but no one I know has ever followed that procedure when using a disposable diaper. Avoiding washing diapers is the reason why most of us choose to use disposables in the first place! Instead, for the sake of convenience, we dump eighty-four million pounds of raw fecal matter into our environment each year, breeding viruses and often contaminating groundwater supplies. There are reasons why we use the modern innovations of sewer systems and wastewater treatment plants, but our insistence on throwing away single-use diapers reeks more of the medieval practice of dumping the chamber pot out the window.

But I confess, I am guilty of all this myself. With my first child I exclusively used disposable diapers. I knew it wasn't the most environmentally friendly choice, but without doing any research, I just used what I thought would be the most convenient option. I had memories of my younger brothers in thin prefold diapers, secured with scarily large pins and covered with uncomfortable vinyl. Having a baby seemed overwhelming enough; I didn't want to deal with hassles like that when easier options were available.

Of course, if I had bothered to look, I would have discovered that cloth diapers have evolved. Today's diapers are well made, easy to use (no pins!) and often made of organic materials.[14] Of course they do require constant washing, but then again, so does everything involving babies! And while there are disposable diapers that avoid dangerous chemicals and decompose faster, these options still pose the issue of multiplying waste (although they are, perhaps, the better option for daycares and church nurseries that require disposables).

However, as my first child potty-trained, I decided to try using cloth diapers with my second child. But then I had to ask myself: Was I willing to make the same decision for myself as I was for my child? While using cloth diapers is still rare, it is still more commonly accepted than reusable sanitary products. Use cloth diapers and you are excused as just caring for your baby (and maybe the environment); use cloth sanitary pads and you are a crunchy, granola, too-far-out-there hippie.

Our culture has fully bought into the advertising claims that if a woman desires to be clean, sanitary, carefree and modern, she has to use disposable sanitary pads. Those lines lured women to buy the first disposable sanitary pads after World War I, as companies frantically sought a market, any market, on which to unload the vast surpluses of cellucotton (used for bandages in the war) in their warehouses.[15] Advertisers told "better-class women" that they had to have this new product, and we women have bought the products ever since.

But as I had decided to put my child in cloth diapers, I surmised that if I also wanted to reduce *my* waste and consumption (and avoid intimate exposure to certain chemicals), I had to at least explore my options. What I discovered were modern, easy-to-use, clean and organic alternatives.[16] After overcoming the years of psychological conditioning, switching over was easy. I had believed the marketing lines that my only options were disposable products, but a little research and a willingness to try new things proved those messages wrong.

Speaking of false messages, back in the late 1980s, reports on the health hazards and environmental dangers of disposable diapers had many states pushing for bans or higher taxes on such items. However, Procter & Gamble (which produces Pampers diapers) launched a massive advertising campaign, claiming that disposable diapers are just as environmentally friendly as cloth diapers. They claimed disposable diapers used less water and were compostable, assertions that were later proved inaccurate and resulted in Procter & Gamble being sued for false advertising.[17] Nevertheless, the millions spent on the advertising campaign had already sent the message to the public. To this day people use this false idea as a rationale for using disposable over cloth diapers. The reality is—if we want to seriously consider the impact we have on this earth, as well as reduce the amount of waste and the dangers of the waste we create—our use of diapers and sanitary products needs rethinking. Choosing the unpopular or slightly less convenient options can have a positive impact on our world.

EVERYDAY PRACTITIONER

Wendy Taylor, mom/teacher
Olympia, Washington

When her son, Liam, was born, Wendy did what nearly every new mother does: bought a mountain of disposable diapers. After four months of struggling with diaper rashes, a friend strongly urged her to look into using cloth diapers. Wendy followed her friend's suggestion, and she soon discovered the serious issues with the disposables she had used without much thought. After some initial hesitation, both Wendy and her husband concluded that cloth diapers were the best option for their family.

With cloth diapers, she was protecting her child, safeguarding the environment and (as she soon discovered) saving money. But for Wendy and her husband, switching to cloth diapers wasn't just a personal decision; it was an act of faith. They believe that God has called everyone to be good stewards of creation, and they desire to abide by that call. Once they understood the negative impact of disposables, they couldn't continue using them in good conscience. As Wendy put it, "preserving our convenience is not more important than preserving God's handiwork."

Since switching to cloth diapers, the only obstacle Wendy has faced is the availability issue. At this point cloth diapers are generally only available online, but as more families choose to return to the environmentally friendly option of cloth diapering, they will probably become more readily available. For the most part Wendy says her friends and family have expressed interest in cloth diapering, and they support her choice. Wendy has even helped other friends make the switch to cloth diapers. Although she has received support for her diapering choice, Wendy admits that she would face greater obstacles if her son was in a daycare center, as these facilities generally refuse to use cloth diapers because they aren't familiar with them. But obstacles like these can be overcome as people like Wendy attempt to educate others about the benefits of cloth diapers.

Nothing could be more everyday than diapers, and for Wendy, using cloth diapers is one way she can live justly in the everyday. She can care for creation and for others with her choice. As she comments on her choice, "I feel confident that we're doing what's best for our son, the environment and our finances. On top of everything else, cloth diapers are really cute!"[18]

CHANGING OUR HABITS

The effects of our disposable habits on both the earth and its inhabitants are devastating. From contaminating water supplies to destroying fields to killing wildlife, our waste is hurting the world. Choosing to love our worldwide neighbors and care for God's creation pushes us to rethink the waste we create. Our addiction to disposable items, our culture's obsession with the cult of the new and our tendency to choose the most convenient option no matter the consequences—these things are difficult to justify when we see the impact our choices have. Becoming aware of the consequences of our actions is only the first step toward helping make things better. Real change occurs after we take the time to start doing things differently. While long-term adjustments in attitude and philosophy may be needed to sustain these changes, I want to suggest three everyday activities to help get us started.

Recycling. Okay, so pretty much everyone has heard of recycling. Most communities across the country offer some sort of recycling service. Recycling can be as simple as sorting potentially recyclable items (generally glass, plastic, paper, aluminum) into boxes you leave on the curb for pick-up. Other communities have drop-off recycling centers or places to return bottles for a deposit. The systems are in place, and all it takes is for us to participate.

Unfortunately even with easy access to recycling outlets, many still choose not to recycle. Citing time, convenience, mess or sheer forgetfulness as excuses, many households simply continue to dump all of their waste into landfills. Take plastic water bottles as an example. These bottles represent the epitome of a disposable society. We pay more for the convenience of what is basically tap water that is prepackaged in potentially toxic, oil-derived plastic. Considering the amount of resources wasted to produce these bottles, we could at least try to keep them from taking over our landfills or oceans. But a 2003 study revealed that only about 12 percent of these bottles in the United States were actually recycled.[19] That means that, every year, billions of bottles end up dumped into the environment. Making a commitment to recycle can be an easy first step to care for the world around us.

However, recycling isn't limited to whatever municipal programs your community provides. Recycling can also mean reusing items that still have life left in them. Learn how to mend your clothes when they tear. Choose to fix appliances instead of just throwing them away. Yes, it may cost about the same to buy new as to repair, but the environmental cost is much less (although replacing an energy-inefficient appliance with one that conserves energy might sometimes be the better option). Instead of throwing away items you no longer need, hold a garage sale or donate them to charity. Be willing to eat leftovers and then compost the food waste you do produce for use in a garden.[20] Or discover the Freecycle Network (freecycle.org) where you can make the items you no longer need or want available for free to whoever wants to pick them up. All of these options require a bit more effort than just tossing stuff in the trash, but they represent a shift from a disposable to a responsible mindset.

Precycling. If recycling focuses on reusing the waste we produce, precycling encourages us to think about how to reduce our waste before we actually create it. By some estimates, every 100 pounds of product we see in stores has already created 3,200 pounds of waste during the manufacturing process.[21] This means every purchase we make has already significantly impacted the environment. Not to mention that most things we buy come with massive amounts of packaging, all of which we usually throw away as soon as we get home. Being aware of the waste our purchases produce may help us rethink what we buy. As you shop, think about the environmental impact of your purchase, and ask yourself a few questions: Do I really need this item? Can I get it used? Is it available to buy in bulk (thereby reducing the packaging)? Is the item made well (which means it may cost more, but it will last longer)? Is having it worth the waste it creates?

PRECYCLING: reducing the production of waste before it is created.

During 2007 I followed the blog of a Canadian woman[22] (known online as EnviroWoman) who tried to take this precycling thing seriously. Given the impact of nonbiodegradable plastic on our environment and our oceans, she committed to live plastic free for at least a year. Her experiment proved harder than she ever expected, prompting weekly confessionals of her plastic-purchase sins (did you know aluminum cans are coated on the inside with plastic?). Her discoveries, struggles and tips on reducing our plastic consumption (and waste) have helped me see that there are options and alternatives to producing so much waste.

In addition to thinking about the items we buy, we can also reduce waste by replacing many of the disposable items we use on a regular basis with reusable alternatives. Choose to refill a stainless steel water bottle instead of reaching for the disposable plastic variety. When shopping, bring your own canvas grocery bags. At

home, get in the habit of using cloth napkins and dishtowels instead of paper towels and napkins. Choose to use real plates and
silverware instead of paper and plastic throwaway options. Use
mugs and real glasses instead of Styrofoam, plastic or paper cups
for drinks at church or in the office. Yes, they require washing, but
as with all these alternatives, a little effort can go a long way toward reducing waste.

Churches can actually lead the way toward everyday justice in
this area. If the church makes the decision to use reusable coffee
mugs and communion cups, for instance, they are setting an example for the church body. Leaders in the church can model
good stewardship by sacrificing time to wash the dishes instead
of just dumping more stuff into landfills. Their example can encourage church members to follow suit, and help solidify the
belief that caring for creation is part of what it means to love
God and love others.

Simplifying. Personally, I've found it easy to integrate recycling
and precycling into my life. It took time, but the changes weren't
that difficult overall. What I'm discovering that is much more difficult, but also vitally important, is simplifying my life and my
consumeristic habits altogether. Habits like recycling often simply
enable a system that tells us we must have more, more, more!
We've fallen for the cult of the new, always having to have the latest, hottest and trendiest items available. We believe that we are
what we consume. The Wal-Mart employee that shoppers trampled to death on Black Friday 2008 illustrates the extent of this
consumeristic obsession in our culture.[23]

We have become a society of rampant consumers. In fact if you
listen to our government, it is our patriotic duty to spend money
and buy more.[24] Such messages are reminiscent of Aldous Huxley's famous anti-utopian work *Brave New World,* which describes
a scene of young children receiving moral training (as dictated by
the government) through sleep hypnosis. After instruction in class

stratification, the lessons turn to developing children into good consumers. The hypnotic whispers repeat the phrases "I do love having new clothes . . . old clothes are beastly . . . we always throw away old clothes. Ending is better than mending."[25]

The irony is that those kinds of extremes aren't even necessary to indoctrinate us into consumeristic lifestyles. Seventy years ago, Huxley still had to combat the mending of clothes as a hindrance to the cult of the new; for most people these days, mending wouldn't even cross their minds. All we need as an excuse to buy more is to want new clothes, or to think our wardrobe is "so last year," or to be told that we deserve new clothes.

I'm not saying we should never buy anything new, but we need to reevaluate the importance we place on "stuff." In Luke's Gospel, Jesus warns against the impulse to acquire and consume, saying, "Watch out! Be on your guard against all kinds of greed; life does not consist in an abundance of possessions" (Lk 12:15). He then encourages his followers to be rich toward God, to not worry about where their clothing or food will come from, and to lay up treasures in heaven instead. His vision of a life focused on trusting God and serving others directly contrasts with the messages received by the children in Huxley's brave new world (and us in our own day), telling them to indulge themselves with more and more. But, honestly, how often do we stop and ask ourselves how much we *really* need?

Earlier in the book, I discussed the need to be an ethical consumer by purchasing fairly produced items, but sometimes the best choice is to simply reduce the amount we consume. As Americans, we use more than our fair share of the earth's resources (and produce more waste as well). As J. Matthew Sleeth puts it, "the earth was designed to sustain every generation's *needs*, not to be plundered to meet one generation's *wants*."[26] Choosing to simplify and reduce our consumption can help us come closer to only taking our fair share of the earth's resources.

Choosing to simplify can also help us break free of the chains greed may hold on our hearts. And breaking away from our desire for more and more stuff can help us sever habits that support the oppression of others. For example, if we reduce the amount of cheap goods (we don't need) that we buy, and if we choose to buy ethically when we do need things (things we will have an easier time affording because we aren't buying so much to begin with), we will not only reduce the amount of waste we produce, we will also reduce the demand for goods made under oppressive conditions.

CONCLUSION

The harm we have done through our waste habits in just the past two centuries is astounding. We already have a continent-sized garbage dump floating on our ocean, a tainted water supply, destroyed fields and inedible fish. We can't trivialize or ignore this damage if we claim to accept God's call to stewardship or if we want to love others (even those we may never meet or who have yet to be born). Taking everyday steps to reduce the damage, and possibly even begin to heal it, will produce a better world.

FOR MORE INFORMATION

Books

Brown, Edward R. *Our Father's World: Mobilizing the Church to Care for Creation.* Downers Grove, Ill.: InterVarsity Press, 2008. A helpful resource that offers a biblical basis for creation care, as well as practical advice for being good stewards.

Royte, Elizabeth. *Garbage Land: On the Secret Trail of Trash.* Boston: Little, Brown and Company, 2005. One woman's exploration of what actually happens to the trash we throw away.

Ryan, John C., and Alan Thein Durning. *Stuff: The Secret Lives of Everyday Things.* Seattle: Northwest Environment Watch, 1997.

Stories about where our stuff comes from and where it ends up.

Strasser, Susan. *Waste and Want: A Social History of Trash*. New York: Metropolitan Books, 1999. A fascinating historical overview of cultural attitudes regarding waste.

Tammemagi, Hans. *The Waste Crisis: Landfills, Incinerators, and the Search for a Sustainable Future*. New York: Oxford University Press, 1999. A detailed examination of the ways we deal with waste and suggestions for better future systems.

Movies

WALL-E. Directed by Andrew Stanton. 98 min., Walt Disney, 2008. An entertaining animated story of the future of an overly consumeristic and wasteful human race.

Websites

Deep Green Conversation
www.deepgreenconversation.org
A Christian resource for sustainable living

The Story of Stuff
www.storyofstuff.com
A twenty-minute online film by Free Range Studios, which traces our consumer habits

Chris Jordan Photography
www.chrisjordan.com
Amazing photo images that represent the magnitude of American consumption

Earth 911
www.earth911.org
A resource site, helping people to recycle and reuse items, and consume responsibly

Debt

PROCLAIMING JUBILEE TO THE NATIONS

Randy looked around at his small group as he pulled a small plastic bag from his pocket. A carpenter by trade, he had just recently returned from Haiti where he had helped construct a new school for some children. Tonight he was sharing his experiences with the group who had supported and prayed for him as he traveled. The trip had ended up being everything and nothing he had expected—touching him in ways he'd never imagined.

As he addressed the group, he showed them the plastic bag, which contained some sort of flat, dry, grayish substance. "I'll pass this around, and I want you to tell me what you think it is," Randy said, handing the bag to the person next to him.

No one ventured a guess as the bag made its way around the circle. A few voices called out for Randy to just tell them already.

"All right," he said. "It's a cookie: a mud and oil cookie that Haitians can buy in the marketplace for next to nothing."

"People eat this?" one group member asked skeptically. "Why?"

"Because they can't afford anything else," Randy replied. "It's heartbreaking, but with the rising cost of food worldwide, many

Haitians can't afford to buy real food. This at least fills their bellies and takes the edge off the hunger. These things are all over the place. It seems that real food is a luxury item."

"But your pictures show a gorgeous tropical island. Can't they grow vegetables or something else to eat?" another member asked.

"They would if political and economic policies hadn't made it impossible," the group leader chimed in. "The Haitians are subject to so many rules and regulations by outside governments and banks that their own economy is devastated. There is very little the people themselves can do to pull themselves out of poverty— which is partly why our church has committed to work down there."

"So the government is basically forcing the people to eat mud cookies?!" one woman exclaimed.

"That's one way of putting it," the leader replied. "It's a long and complicated story, but one I hope we can help change by sending people like Randy down there, and by working for change here in the States. We just have to be willing to get involved."

☞

Imagine for a minute that someone stole your wallet. After the initial panic, you'd start canceling your credit cards, hoping to ward off fraudulent charges. Besides having to deal with the hassle, though, everything will generally work out just fine. Now imagine, instead, that before you were even born, someone stole your credit card, charged ten billion dollars in weapons on it and is requiring you to pay it all back with interest. The hardship of being forced to pay back those charges results in you not having clean water, in health services not being available to you and in your children not being able to even attend school.

This may seem like a farcical scenario to the average American. As Americans, we want life to be fair, and suffering for debts we didn't incur isn't the way we expect the world to work. When we hear the term *debt,* we tend to think of our maxed-out credit cards. Debt in our country often has the stigma of poor personal choices and greed attached to it. We believe that debt is personal and must be personally paid off. So naturally some confusion arises when the topic of international debt, or Third World debt as it's often called, comes up.

WHAT IS THIRD WORLD DEBT?

To give a very basic introduction, Third World debt describes the millions of dollars in debt that countries have incurred from loans from other countries, from the International Monetary Fund (IMF) and from the World Bank. These loans were (at least theoretically) intended to help the country. The problem is that many of these loans were either irresponsibly given, acquired (and squandered) illegally by dictators, or are the remains of colonialism and the Cold War. These are debts that the people of these countries didn't ask for or approve of (like South Africans having to pay back the loans that the apartheid government took and used to fight anti-apartheid efforts, for instance), and now some countries have to use up to 80 percent of their national budgets to repay these debts and their insane interest rates.

To repay debts these countries have cut public education and health services, and stopped hiring doctors, nurses and teachers.[1] Even the humanitarian aid given to struggling countries often simply gets returned to the wealthier countries in the form of debt repayment. The interest rates on the loans are so extreme that many countries see no end to giving away all their money to wealthy Western nations and banks. To take just one example: Nigeria has borrowed five billion dollars, and to date, it has paid back sixteen billion dollars, but it still owes thirty-two billion dollars. There are a number of reasons why these debts are wrong, but the ultimate effect of them is that they are keeping the poorest countries in this world in cycles of extreme poverty. Many of the justice issues mentioned in this book connect in some way to debt. To truly understand the causes of these injustices, we have to first understand this debt and what it does to countries.

Take the example of Haiti. By some standards, Haiti is the poorest country in the world. The economy is devastated and the 2008 protests over the cost of food revealed that many citizens eat mud cookies in an attempt to suppress hunger. Political unrest (often due to these economic issues) has even halted much of the charity work in the country. While my own church has partnered with groups in Haiti, hosting charity dinners to fund and sending work teams to construct schools and clinics in a specific region,[2] it is necessary to see the bigger picture and understand the roots of Haiti's economic issues—roots based in exploitation, oppression and debt.

Of any country in the New World, Haiti has the longest history of exploitation. In 1492, Columbus established a military outpost in Haiti, and within decades, disease, slavery and outright slaughter had wiped out the native Taino population. By the late eighteenth century, Europeans were bringing over roughly twenty-nine thousand slaves a year from Africa to work in the gold mines and newly established plantations.[3] Eventually Spain ceded control of the region to France, who continued to use slave labor to prosper their interests in Haiti.

In 1804 these slaves staged the first successful slave rebellion in history—overthrowing their French oppressors, establishing the country of Haiti and becoming the first country in the world to abolish slavery. Fearful of seeing similar revolts on their own soil, almost all of the world's nations refused to recognize the sovereignty of Haiti or trade with them. In 1825, aided by U.S. money and troops, the king of France sent a fleet of ships to retake the country. Faced with superior military might, the Haitians agreed to a treaty, by which they retained their freedom (and had France officially recognize them as a nation) but had to pay restitution of

150 million francs (the equivalent of $21 billion today) for France's loss of revenue from slave labor.[4] With no countries willing to trade with them and facing crippling debt, Haiti struggled to develop and thrive from its very beginnings as an independent, postcolonial nation.

In 1914, fearing French and German influence in Haiti as World War I commenced, U.S. Marines invaded Haiti and stole the nation's currency, thereby gaining control of Haiti's finances. While U.S. lenders assumed the notes for the debt, the military guaranteed repayment by forcefully controlling Haiti's government and treasury. For nearly twenty years while the U.S. military occupied the country, Haitian taxes were sent directly to the United States, and forced labor was used to strip the country of many of its natural resources (especially Haiti's mahogany forests). Resource-laden Haitian land was given away to U.S. businesses with little regard for the Haitian inhabitants. When Haitians protested this practice, Marines killed between three thousand (U.S. reports) and fifteen thousand (Haitian reports) displaced peasants.[5] Needless to say, this theft of Haitian resources prevented Haiti from establishing itself as a self-sufficient nation. After the U.S. withdrew in 1934, the country was left in ecological and economic ruin, controlled by dictators who acquired even more debt for the country. Stripped of its forests, Haiti has suffered massive landslides and flooding over the years, and its economy has continued in a downward spiral as the ongoing effects of debt trap it in cycles of poverty.

While Haiti continues to suffer the centuries-old effects of colonialism, other debt crises around the world are mostly a product of the last fifty years. During the 1960s, there was a surplus of oil money around the world. Banks need to lend money in order to make money through interest, so, faced with a monetary surplus and plummeting interest rates, Western banks desperately offered loans to Third World countries. Most of these countries had decent economies, but they wanted the low-interest loans to help build infrastructure (although, on some occasions, the loans were taken for corrupt leaders' personal use, but the banks weren't too picky about such things).

Circumstances converged in the 1970s to prompt a crisis. Many developing countries had been advised by the West to improve their economies by growing cash crops for export. Unfortunately, too many countries received the same advice, and these cash crops flooded the market, causing prices to fall. Then interest rates rose. Many Third World countries found themselves earning very little for their exports and having to pay ever-increasing interest on their loans. Some countries even had to acquire other loans just to pay the interest on the loans they already had.

In 1982 Mexico was the first country to default on its loans. As a U.S. Treasury Department official put it, "the Mexican Minister of Finance showed up at our doorstep and turned his pockets inside out."[6] As other countries also began defaulting, the International Monetary Fund (IMF) and World Bank came to their "rescue" with new loans that came with some serious strings attached. These strings required governments to impose very strict economic programs in their countries. While these programs were designed to increase income for the country, they often came at the expense of everyday life for the average person living there. Some of the rules required governments to spend less on health, education and social services, to cut back on food subsidies, and to force farmers to grow cash crops for export instead of staple foods for consumption. As a result, some nations in Africa now spend four times as much on debt repayment than on health care. To put numbers to it, some estimate that Africa needs $15 billion annually to fight HIV/AIDS, yet African nations pay out $13.5 billion in debt repayment each year.[7]

The history and magnitude of this debt are overwhelming. And while these grand schemes that are played out on the global scale are often difficult to grasp, we should remember as we encounter these stories that it is often the poorest people in these countries who suffer the most because of their country's debt. They are the ones crying out for justice.

THE CONSEQUENCES OF DEBT

When countries are forced to funnel their meager resources into debt repayment, other national interests are left to fall by the wayside. Sometimes these consequences are the direct result of stipulations enforced by the World Bank and the IMF, and sometimes they are just what the country must do to survive. Government programs like education, health care and public works systems (water, electricity, road maintenance) are often the first eliminated in favor of debt repayment. With little to no government-subsidized health care, for example, those who cannot afford to pay for health care must simply go without. Countries whose health care improved with scientific advances early in the twentieth century watched those improvements dwindle away after certain loan stipulations reduced their country's health-care budget. Since the debt crisis began, child death rates increased, and diseases once thought to be eradicated returned to the heavily indebted countries due to lack of vaccines. For example, government immunization cutbacks in the state of São Paulo, Brazil, led to a measles epidemic that killed thousands of babies.[8]

Similar stories abound in the sphere of education. Universal public education is a luxury often taken for granted by wealthy nations. When the government cannot provide free education, schools must charge fees. Education is then only available to those wealthy enough to pay for it. One effect of this is the widening of the gender gap around the world. In cultures that value boys more than girls, a family will not "waste" precious resources to pay for a girl to attend school. The result is generations of illiterate, uneducated women—a dangerous situation since women generally make the nutritional and medical decisions for their families.

World Bank and IMF requirements also force many countries to privatize public water services. Instead of being a basic human right that is available to all, water is controlled by large businesses that are required by these rules to make a profit. Once the supply is privatized and access to it is heavily controlled, some families find that they can no longer afford clean water. Others find themselves unable to get clean water at all, because the companies will cut the water supply to poor, rural areas where they can't make a profit.

In Ghana, water privatization, required by the World Bank, resulted in a 95 percent rate increase for water. As a result many families have to spend up to 20 percent of their income on water.[9] For some who are barely getting by as it is, paying for clean water just isn't an option. But without clean water, diseases flourish— claiming children as their main victims. Others recognize that water is necessary for life and isn't a commodity that can be abandoned, so they have no choice but to pay these prices they can ill afford. Even those who choose to pay, though, have difficulty accessing the water supply. Globally, women spend an average of eight hours per day, traveling as far as fifteen kilometers, to gather some fifteen to twenty liters of water.[10] This extra toil comes at the expense of education and income-generating work. It is hard to end cycles of poverty with constraints as basic as water supply holding people back.

Other effects of the debt crisis make it hard for some to even survive day to day. Remember the food riots in the streets of Port-au-Prince, Haiti, in the spring of 2008? While the world watched with pity and sent charity, some people asked why Haitians weren't just growing their own food or working harder to make more money to buy food. In the United States (where even the poorest rarely spend more than 16 percent of their income on food), it is hard to imagine the struggle that those people, who already spend 50 to 75 percent on food, face when world food prices rise by nearly 40 percent.[11] For the Haitians, this means they could no longer even afford rice, a staple of their diet. While their president quickly subsidized the cost of rice in Haiti—providing some relief—to fully understand the crisis we need to look at how debt led them to this point in the first place.

Although Haiti used to internally produce all the rice it needed, that all changed because of stipulations imposed by the IMF in the 1980s. After the dictator Jean Claude "Baby Doc" Duvalier was ousted (after he bankrupted the treasury), Haiti received loans from the IMF to help rebuild. However, the strings attached to these loans required Haiti to drop subsidies and lower tariff protection on crops like rice, and also open up their markets to more imports like heavily subsidized U.S. rice. Without the tariffs, or duty tax, placed on the import of U.S. rice, it quickly started pouring into the country and flooding the Haitian markets. Within a couple of years, Haitian farmers discovered that they couldn't compete with the cheaper rice from the United States and found themselves out of work. While the IMF claimed that this system would help Haiti compete in a free market economy, the local farmers saw that barely taxed rice from the United States, which sold cheaply because the government subsidized it, always dominated their heavily taxed, unsubsidized crops. Healthy competition on the free market requires a semblance of equality; Haiti though didn't stand a chance against an economic giant like the United States. But as rice prices have risen dramatically (114 percent in just 2007), the Haitians find themselves unable to buy foreign rice and with no local options left to turn to.

In 2007 my husband, Mike, spent time working with missionaries in Haiti, attempting to alleviate some of the most severe effects of poverty. Mike commented that while he could build schools and help some families, finding comprehensive solutions to end poverty in Haiti would be difficult. Without a healthy economic infrastructure, Haiti's numerous broken systems—from schools, to roads, to clinics, to electricity and water—cannot be fixed, only patched here and there with occasional charity work. Mike saw firsthand the good that charity can achieve, but he also realized the need to work for systemic healing for the country as a whole. Debt caused the crisis for which there is no quick solution. But justice is always possible.

JUBILEE

The solution many propose for the worldwide debt crisis is actually a biblical one: forgiveness of debts. The proposal is that nations, the World Bank and the IMF should cancel the debts of impoverished countries in order to free up resources to help those countries rebuild and heal. Many of those debts, acquired by dictators and pushed on struggling nations, are of a highly dubious nature. When banks give loans to fund the personal greed of dictators (as with the Duvaliers in Haiti), or when a government pushes a loan on another country to further its own interest (like the United States loaning weapon-development funding to various countries during the Cold War, in order to prevent them from turning communist), and then those loans ruin a country, one has to question the ethical basis of the loan to begin with. In addition, many of these countries have already paid the principal on these debts, but the interest payments are keeping them in poverty. As with Haiti, even after throwing off the chains of physical slavery, the people are still enslaved because debt limits their country's development. In response to these debt crises, politicians, economists and religious leaders have joined forces to call for the cancellation of Third World debt—or to use the biblical term, to proclaim "jubilee."

In the year of jubilee, the enslaved are set free, debtors' debts are forgiven, and community that is fractured by inequality is restored.

Leviticus 25 describes the year of jubilee. Acknowledging that all resources ultimately belong to God, every fiftieth year the Israelites were to set aside that year as holy to the Lord. During this year they were to plant no crops and were to right economic relationships. In the year of jubilee, land returned to its original owner, slaves were set free, and debts were forgiven. In this way God ensured that all his people had equal economic opportunity and that they would escape the trap where the rich get richer while the poor spiral deeper into poverty. Every fiftieth year the playing field leveled in a holy year dedicated to the Lord. In light of crippling Third World debt, many believe that the world needs a modern-day jubilee.

We can find support for continuing this practice of jubilee in the words of Jesus himself. As I mentioned earlier, in his inaugural sermon, Jesus proclaimed,

> The Spirit of the Lord is on me,
>> because he has anointed me
>> to proclaim good news to the poor.
> He has sent me to proclaim freedom for the prisoners
>> and recovery of sight for the blind,
> to set the oppressed free,
>> to proclaim the year of the Lord's favor. (Lk 4:18-19)

The actions Jesus refers to here echo the requirements of the year of jubilee, and many scholars believe that "the year of the Lord's favor" is another term for jubilee.[12] Jesus devoted much of his teaching to encouraging others to make jubilee a reality. Those of us accustomed to a spiritualized reading of the Gospels often overlook the everyday applications that were there for Jesus' original listeners. In the familiar words of the Lord's Prayer, where Jesus taught his disciples to pray, he told them to ask for God's kingdom to be made known on earth and for debts to be forgiven. While some translations refer to "debts" as "sins" or "trespasses" instead, the

Greek word used there refers specifically to monetary debt, strengthening the call to cancel debts as the jubilee year required.[13] Similarly in the parables in Matthew 18:21-35 (the unmerciful servant) and Luke 16:1-14 (the shrewd manager), Jesus praises those who cancel the monetary (and often unjust) debts of others. In a cultural setting where the poor often became nearly slaves because of the debt that was caused by the crippling taxes of Rome, Herod and the temple, this message of jubilee gave them hope.

The call for a modern-day jubilee looks to the debt-related oppression of millions around the world and asks that the ruling political and economic powers cancel it. The struggle of so many just to survive, combined with the biblical impetus to forgive debts, has sparked a worldwide jubilee movement. Establishing the year of 2000 as a year of jubilee, campaigns to drop the debt gained momentum in the mid-1990s. By the time my husband and I traveled through Europe in the summer of 2000, it seemed like every church and cathedral had a Jubilee 2000 petition displayed for us to sign. The campaign "gained clout from the 24 million signatures on its petitions, and endorsements from Pope John Paul II, the Dalai Lama, and U2 lead singer Bono,"[14] achieving spectacular results.

The jubilee campaign made lawmakers and world leaders aware of the need for and validity of debt cancellation. World leaders made promises in 1998, 2000 and 2005 regarding partial debt cancellation, and even these partial cancellations have resulted in significant change. After the relief of their debt, Tanzania was able to eliminate school fees, and 1.5 million children returned to school almost overnight. In Mozambique, nearly 500,000 children received vaccinations. But many countries have yet to see any relief from debt or are still constrained by restrictive rules that prevent help from getting to the people who need it most.

This is why groups around the world continue to call on governments to increase the numbers of debts canceled and to do so without harmful strings attached. Concerned citizens still implore their leaders to make debt a priority and to seek jubilee. Many echo Desmond Tutu's words: "shall we let the children of Africa and Asia die of curable disease, prevent them from going to school and limit their opportunities for meaningful work—all to pay off unjust and illegitimate loans made to their forefathers?"[15] The situation looks hopeful as the U.S. House of Representatives approved the *Jubilee Act* (H.R. 2634) in April 2008 (as of early 2009, it was still pending a Senate vote). This act would expand the number of countries eligible for debt relief and would ensure that monies saved will target poverty reduction. The possibility that the "year of the Lord's favor" will actually bring freedom to those oppressed by debt is becoming a reality.

OTHER REASONS TO SEEK DEBT RELIEF

Beyond just taking responsibility for our country's complicity in contributing to Third World debt, there are other reasons why forgiving debts is something that should concern U.S. citizens. While proclaiming jubilee is part of seeking justice and is a moral issue that people of faith should care about, sometimes it can be easy to see this issue as other people's problems. But the debt crisis isn't just somebody else's problem; it can affect each of us on a personal level. We are all interconnected: how we treat our neighbor affects the entire world, and how we treat the world can come back to affect our family and friends.

Health concerns feature prominently in the rationale for debt cancellation. In many countries the government controls the medical infrastructure, and as indebted countries slash funds to health services, disease flourishes. Private companies can provide such services, but in poorer countries there isn't much incentive for privatized medicine, which can't make a profit. Nonprofit organizations do provide some services, but there often isn't enough charity to cover all the needs. So when governments are strapped for cash because of high debt repayments, the medical system dwindles. Without clinics to treat disease, even common ailments turn deadly. There is already a significant rise in easily preventable diseases in debt-plagued countries, and it is a direct result of the reduction in doctors, nurses and clinics.

Countries where treatable diseases devastate the population often do not have the ability to pull together to help themselves. There are basic quality-of-life standards, such as clean water, that must be met before progress in health care can be made. Beyond the tragedy of people suffering (and dying) from preventable diseases, there is also the potential for deadly diseases to proliferate, affecting the entire world. Early and easily accessible medical care can help prevent the spread of epidemics. Deadly diseases can be isolated and treated in swift fashion. But in areas without access to medical facilities, deadly diseases spread rapidly. Epidemics of TB or avian flu, for example, could potentially affect the whole world. Early detection and treatment of disease are necessary to protect neighbors and ourselves from medical disaster. But this requires funding in impoverished countries, and currently, that money is being channeled into debt repayment instead. Freeing up that money for medical infrastructure can help keep the world safe.

Debt relief is similarly linked to the environment. As the countries that spend 80 percent of their budgets on debt repayment scramble to find alternate sources of income, environmental abuse increases. To survive, people cut clear entire forests, plant unsustainable crops, overuse pesticides and improperly dispose of chemicals in rivers. These practices destroy ecosystems and will eventually result in a completely unlivable landscape. Desperate attempts to save or make a buck right now, attempts that do not consider the long-term costs, will only lead to greater problems in the future.

When the land has been devastated by overuse of chemicals and unsustainable practices, what will be left for the people to farm? Where will they grow food? If the land can no longer support the people, they will need the support and charity of others as they attempt to find new land to live off of. The world has already seen food riots in places like Haiti that can no longer sustain their own needs. In the search for food and land, the world will see both a flood of immigrants (both legal and illegal) and an increase in violent attempts to take these things from others. And the cost of solutions will eventually be much higher than the cost of developing sustainable practices right now. The catch is that, for countries to develop such practices in the here and now, resources must be available to help make that happen. Countries whose debt repayments consume resources have no ability to take those steps. Debt cancellation helps stabilize economies, which provides the space for sustainable practices to flourish.

Finally, debt cancellation has a role to play when it comes to national security. Nations where the government and economy are not stable enough to provide basic necessities for the people (medical systems, access to food, education) often face higher levels of civil unrest. Unstable countries pose threats to more prosperous countries around the world. Sometimes this takes the form of direct invasion as one country seeks to overtake the resources of another. More often, though, this unrest provides the breeding ground for terrorist activity. For example, as Pakistan's economy crumbled and they took loans from the IMF, education suffered. Children didn't have access to schools or to education that would teach them how to think critically about their world. Then the Taliban stepped in. Amidst poverty and a generation of children looking for guidance, the Taliban set up thousands of *madrassas* (religious schools), which offered not only education but free room and board.[16] What the government was unable to provide to desperate families, the Taliban was more than willing to provide in ways that assured them well-trained disciples. It is far easier for extreme ideologies to take root when there are no alternatives to choose from.[17] Removing the conditions that foster terrorism seems like a logical step toward our own national security. Relieving the debt of countries so they can care for their own is part of improving those conditions.

YOUR ROLE IN DEBT RELIEF

At this point you may be excited about the possibility of debt relief but have no idea how that relates to your everyday life. Debt relief seems like such a large-scale issue—something for governments, economists and lawmakers to handle. *How can one person ever effect change on such a big issue?* you may wonder. To assure you that debt relief is very much an everyday justice issue, let me tell you a story about two soccer moms from Alabama.

Pat Pelham and Elaine Van Cleave of Birmingham, Alabama, first heard about global hunger needs and debt relief at a church Bible study. Amazed that such conditions exist in the world today, they became actively involved in local awareness and relief projects. Wanting to spread the word about these issues, they invited their congressional representative, Spencer Bachus, to attend a hunger-awareness fundraising banquet, where they encouraged him to support legislation to fight the causes of hunger around the world. The two women, overwhelmed by the thought of "ordinary moms" speaking to a politician, were even more shocked when Representative Bachus contacted them after the event. Moved by what he had heard, he told them, "I doubt that this will win me many votes, but I don't want to be responsible for even one child going hungry."[18] So he began to speak out for justice.

Pat and Elaine continued to raise awareness of the need for debt relief as it related to ending hunger. Elaine said that, as a mother, she found it upsetting that children around the world die of preventable causes. "If I had to choose between paying a debt that I had inherited from my parents and buying food for my children, the choice would be clear." So she and Pat gathered signatures, made their way to Washington, D.C., and followed up with Representative Bachus to encourage him to support debt relief legislation. Bachus, a devout Southern Baptist, had his eyes opened to justice issues because of the involvement of "church people" back home. He introduced bipartisan legislation like the *Jubilee Act* in June 2007, and he committed to using his political career to help end suffering in the world.

Hearing Pat and Elaine tell their story at a Jubilee USA conference inspired me. They expressed their amazement that they, as ordinary people, could help bring about significant change. While they could have assumed that, as busy soccer moms, they could never have much effect on world hunger and debt relief, their convictions as Christians and their empathy as mothers wouldn't allow them to do nothing. And instead, they saw how ordinary people can work within their everyday lives to effect great change. For them that involved the two-step process of raising awareness and political involvement.

Awareness. Awareness is a necessary first step in working for change. Knowing how our choices affect the world around us can help us move toward making better choices. Yet there are actually very few people out there who are aware of problems like Third World debt. Activists and politicians may talk about these things, but it usually takes hearing about them from a trusted friend for everyday people to really listen. Talking to friends at church or inviting a coworker to an awareness banquet can often be the most effective way to spread the word.

Activism. Beyond raising awareness, there are some issues that require Americans to exercise their right to a political voice. Issues like debt relief are really big. They play out on a global scale, and their terms are dictated by world governments. Most of the problems with debt were created by governments and, therefore, require political solutions. So seeking everyday justice will sometimes require getting politically involved—being a voice for the voiceless, talking to those who have the power to affect these people's lives.

Unfortunately many Christians and advocates for justice are wary of politics and politicians. Many are turned off by the moral compromises of politics, and they prefer to work for change on a much smaller scale by helping one person at a time. While I understand this perspective and applaud that work, I also firmly believe that political involvement is a necessary step in some situations. *And* it's something the ordinary person can easily do.

CONCLUSION

Working for change on a small scale is always good and necessary, but large-scale issues should not be ignored either. We don't have to choose between one or the other but should, instead, actively seek to love God and others in a multitude of ways. Helping out at a local food pantry or tutoring struggling students in your community are great ways to demonstrate love for others. But helping to ensure that people around the world have access to affordable food and education is needed as well. It can be easy to help meet the needs of the person right in front of you and then believe that global problems can never be resolved, just as it is possible to work at raising awareness for global issues without ever meeting with the suffering people just down the street. Seeking justice means choosing to do so for all.

Through our votes and through our continued communication with our elected officials, we can have an impact on global justice issues. However, this requires actually letting our representatives know what we care about. As Pat and Elaine discovered, any citizen has the right to meet with, call or write their elected officials. And these officials are paid to listen (that's their job). Knowing that helping children around the world attend school and have access to basic health services is a concern of their constituents actually helps politicians make decisions. So when you are aware of justice issues under consideration by the government (like the *Jubilee Act*), take the time to encourage your representative to support those issues. Democracy works by letting your voice be heard.

On the issue of debt relief, Jubilee USA (www.jubileeusa.org) is a helpful resource and organizing force. From providing resources for churches and schools to organizing conferences to pushing legislation and coordinating letter-writing campaigns, Jubilee USA seeks to do whatever they can to end Third World debt. If you are interested in getting more involved with debt relief, visiting their website will direct you to the multiple, everyday ways you can help bring about change and start proclaiming jubilee.

FOR MORE INFORMATION

Books

Roodman, David Malin. *Still Waiting for the Jubilee: Pragmatic Solutions for the Third World Debt Crisis.* Washington, D.C.: Worldwatch Institute, 2001. A historic overview of international debt and potential solutions to the problem.

Vallely, Paul. *Bad Samaritans: First World Ethics and Third World Debt.* Maryknoll, N.Y.: Orbis Books, 1990. An exploration of the debt crisis, which encourages people to move from charity to justice.

Movies

Bamako. Written and directed by Abderrahmane Sissako. 117 min., New Yorker Video, 2006. A critically acclaimed political drama, where the citizens of Bamako, Mali, hold international financial organizations accountable for many of Africa's problems.

Life and Debt. Produced and directed by Stephanie Black. 80 min., New Yorker Video, 2001. A sobering look at how international debt has changed the economy and people of Jamaica.

Websites

DATA (Debt, AIDS, Trade, Africa)
www.data.org
An advocacy organization focusing on eliminating the causes of poverty in Africa

Jubilee USA
www.jubileeusa.org
A resource site providing educational materials and activism suggestions related to international debt issues

USA.gov
www.usa.gov/Contact/Elected.shtml
Information about how to contact your elected representatives

Conclusion

During the process of writing this book, I often encountered the attitude that seeking justice and trying to change the world is just too hard. It might be fine for some radicals, but the average person, for whatever reason, just can't do it. Some blame this sort of attitude on the overwhelming nature of the problems and the abundance of good causes demanding our attention. Others lay the blame on our cultural "Santa Clausification"[1] of those who commit their lives to seeking justice. Civil rights leaders like Martin Luther King Jr., or charity workers like Mother Teresa, are portrayed in such saintly terms that they seem almost super-human (like Santa Claus). Their everyday humanity is hidden, and all we see are their extreme sacrifices for good. This kind of portrayal causes the average person to think (as comedian Stephen Colbert put it), "There was a great man. No *way* I could do what he did."[2] The unfortunate result is that we come to see loving others as something for other people to do.

AS INDIVIDUALS

Yet the command to love is given to all. I hope this book has been a helpful resource as you think through what that call to action will look like in your life. Like I mentioned earlier: *Don't panic.*

Choose a few ways you can seek justice in the everyday. Maybe that is all you'll ever do, or perhaps it is merely a place for you to start. This will play out differently depending on each of our individual life's circumstances. I encourage you, however, to go beyond what I have written here. This book is, in many ways, just an introduction. The issues brought up and the suggestions given represent a small segment of the numerous ways that we can help make the world a better place. These are places to start.

I hope I've helped make you more aware of the ways our day-to-day actions affect the world around us. Living for just ourselves isn't an option, because *everything* we do impacts other people. It is up to us to decide whether we will act lovingly toward others or whether we will participate in their exploitation and harm. *How* we choose to put love into practice will vary for each person, but I hope these choices are ones we can no longer simply ignore.

My friends and family who answer the call to seek justice do so in a myriad of ways. My friend Karen seeks out ethically made clothing to wear. My retired father, formerly a water engineer, travels to Mexico to drill wells and build bathhouses in the impoverished shantytowns, providing the people there with much-needed clean water. My mother, whose rare blood is safe to give newborn babies requiring immediate transfusions, has regularly donated blood for the last fifteen years. My friend Jen spends her free time assisting the homeless. My aunt runs an environmentally conscious cattle ranch. My friend Erin lived in a hut over the ocean in Panama for two years, working with the Peace Corps to help local people develop sustainable farming practices. Seeking justice looks different in each of their lives, but they are each doing what they can to answer that call.

Christians should care about these things because they are things that God cares about. We are called to seek first the kingdom of God (Mt 6:33)—including the call to love God and love others (Mt 22:37-39). As author Richard Foster writes in his classic work *Celebration of Discipline*, "when the kingdom of God is genuinely placed first, ecological concerns, the poor, the equitable distribution of wealth, and many other things will be given their proper attention."[3] Making a difference with these issues should just be an everyday part of what it means to be a Christ-follower. God created and called us to do good works. Ephesians reminds us that we have been saved by grace so that we can do good works (Eph 2:8-10). This is not a duty we have or a passion we develop; it is a destiny we were born to fulfill.

I am encouraged by reading 1 Corinthians 15, where this call is tied to the hope we have in Jesus. This chapter explores the resurrection and how we are saved from death through Jesus. It details the hope we have in the bodily resurrection when all things are made new. In light of that hope, we are told "Therefore, my dear brothers and sisters, stand firm. Let nothing move you. Always give yourselves fully to the work of the Lord, because you know that your labor in the Lord is not in vain" (1 Cor 15:58). Our response to the hope we have for eternity is to commit ourselves to working for God in the here and now, knowing that what we do has eternal significance.

AS A COMMUNITY

Seeking justice in the everyday, though, is not something we do alone. As the Talmud, a collection of rabbinic writings, said, "It is not upon you to complete the task, but you are not free to idle from it."[4] We are responsible to act, but it is not up to us to complete the task, so we shouldn't feel overwhelmed or pressured or guilty. The fate of the world doesn't rest on our shoulders. We are simply trying to follow Jesus and, for that, we have been promised aid.

Standing with us as we live justly are the Holy Spirit and our communities of faith. It is within the strength and support of these relationships that we serve. We don't have to (and shouldn't) trust in our own strength and commitment, but instead accept this en-

couragement, accountability and support. The early church knew
all about trusting in the Holy Spirit and accepting others' support.
The Holy Spirit came among them and empowered them to continue in Christ's work, and they met together daily for encouragement and prayer. In Acts 4, we find them earnestly asking in prayer
for boldness in doing the work of the Lord. Immediately their
prayers were answered and

> they were all filled with the Holy Spirit and spoke the word of
> God boldly. All the believers were one in heart and mind. No
> one claimed that any of their possessions was their own, but
> they shared everything they had. With great power the apos-
> tles continued to testify to the resurrection of the Lord Jesus.
> And God's grace was so powerfully at work in them all that
> there were no needy persons among them. (Acts 4:31-34)

Together they cared for each other's needs through the power of
the Holy Spirit. They weren't just individuals, trying to make sense
of what it means to seek justice and follow Jesus each by themselves; this was something they did as a community. Having the
support of a community helps all of us better commit to seeking
justice.

As you finish this book, I'd encourage you to seek out this kind
of support. Don't try to accomplish the things mentioned here in
your own strength. Find others to walk alongside you in the process. Discover groups where you can seek everyday justice in community. Where you can help each other find resources or share
ideas about living simply. Where you can start a garden with a
friend or visit your local congressional representative together.
Where you can find encouragement when you feel overwhelmed
and motivation when you become apathetic.

Community like this is vital to the work of justice. No one can
do this alone. Justice is done in the name of, by the power of and
in the community of Jesus.

So don't panic. No need to feel overwhelmed or wary. Find friends. Trust Jesus. And. Seek. Justice.

Loving God and loving others every day can be that simple.

And that extreme.

Acknowledgments

I wish this book didn't exist—or more precisely that it didn't have to exist. If injustices didn't abound in the world today then there would be no need for this book. But, unfortunately, there are stories of pain and suffering that must be told, that we need to do something about. So it is somewhat bittersweet for me to thank those who helped me tell those stories and make this book a reality.

First, thank you to authors like Brian McLaren, Tony Campolo, Brian Walsh, Tom Sine, Jim Wallis and Shane Claiborne for waking me up to the reality that justice is a faith issue. Thank you to Karen Sloan for making me promise to share what I'd learned about these issues with others. Thank you, Sarah and Ryan Notton, for creating the "Julie Clawson Should Write a Book" Facebook group and pushing me to just do it already. Thank you to the communities at Emergent Village and Emerging Women who encouraged me to use my voice. Thank you to all my friends at Via Christus who helped me discover this stuff in community—I miss you guys. And, because I always said I would thank her if I ever wrote a book, thank you to Martha Druce, my third-grade teacher, for believing in me and encouraging me to write.

Thank you Alexa, Wendy, Josh and David for being willing to share your stories. And thank you to the hundreds of others who are standing up every day for justice. You encourage me to keep believing that there is good in this world that's worth fighting for.

Thank you to all the fantastic people at InterVarsity Press who helped turn this book into a reality. Thank you, Andrew Bronson, Adrianna Wright and Elaina Whittenhall, for your enthusiasm, encouragement and support. And, especially, thank you to my editor, Al Hsu, for giving me the opportunity to tell these stories, for helping me navigate through the controversial parts and for being willing to answer my endless questions.

And my deepest thanks to my family. Thank you, Mom (Nana) for watching the kids so I could have a few quiet moments to write. To Emma, who understands that sometimes "mommies write books and Nanas paint toenails," and to Aidan who gestated and came to life alongside this book; thank you for your trust and love—I hope, as you grow, we can work for justice together. And to my husband, Mike, thank you for your unfailing support, for those nights when you attempted to make dinner so I could write just a little bit longer, for reading through every single draft of this book and for imagining with me a better world.

Notes

Warning!

[1]George L. Rogers, ed., *Benjamin Franklin's The Art of Virtue: His Formula for Successful Living* (Eden Prairie, Minn.: Acorn, 1996), p. 41.

[2]Ibid., p. 43.

Introduction

[1]Sudan is the world's leading exporter of gum arabic, providing up to 90 percent of the world's supply. This substance, derived from the acacia tree, is prevalent in many candies and soft drinks. In 1997 when the atrocities in Sudan started to be publicly known and words like *genocide* were proposed, the "gum arabic lobby" formed to oppose planned U.S. sanctions against Sudan. The sanctions passed, but the gum arabic lobby (funded by, among others, The National Soft Drink Association) pushed for and obtained an exception allowing for the continued export of gum arabic, despite Sudan's Gum Arabic Company's connection to known terrorist Osama bin Laden. This essentially made the sanctions meaningless since they no longer had the economic impact to pressure involved parties to end the violence. In 2007 the Sudanese ambassador John Ukec Lueth, in protest of new U.S. sanctions, threatened to take away the world's Coca-Cola by halting gum arabic export if the world didn't stop insisting that there were killings occurring in Darfur. (See Thomas W. Lippman, "Threatened Ban on Key Import Has Lobbyists Lining Up Behind Sudan Trade," *Washington Post,* October 16, 1997 <www.highbeam.com/doc/1P2-752634.html>; and Russell

Goldman, "Flapping Their Gum: Sudan Threatens U.S. Soft Drinks," *ABC News,* June 1, 2007 <http://abcnews.go.com/US/story?id= 3232434>.)

[2]Dictionary.com, s.v. "justice" <http://dictionary.reference.com/browse/ justice>.

[3]Scot McKnight, *A Community Called Atonement* (Nashville: Abingdon, 2007), p. 19.

[4]*Call+Response,* prod. and dir. Justin Dillon, 86 min., Fair Trade Pictures, 2008, DVD.

[5]*Online Etymology Dictionary,* s.v. "justice" <www.etymonline.com/ index.php?term=justice>.

[6]I found all the book and movie resources mentioned at my local library through the nationwide interlibrary loan system (excepting those still in theaters as of this writing). Most are also available for purchase or rent through online sources like Amazon.com and Netflix.com.

Chapter 1: Coffee

[1]Oxfam International, Make Trade Fair site, "Real Lives: Coffee," <www .maketradefair.com/en/index.php?file=issues_coffee.htm>.

[2]Paul Jeffrey, "Depressed Coffee Prices Yield Suffering in Poor Countries," *National Catholic Reporter* online, February 7, 2003 <http:// natcath.org/NCR_Online/archives2/2003a/020703/020703a.htm>.

[3]Oxfam International, "Bitter Coffee: How the Poor Are Paying for the Slump in Coffee Prices" <www.globalexchange.org/campaigns/fairtrade/ coffee/OxfamPriceReport.pdf>.

[4]Alex Renton, "This Is a Story About Gourmet Coffee and Genocide. It Takes Place in Rwanda . . . ," *The Observer,* February 25, 2007 <http:// observer.guardian.co.uk/foodmonthly/story/0,,2017481,00.html>.

[5]Oxfam International, "Real Lives: Coffee."

[6]Oxfam International, Make Trade Fair site, "Mugged: Poverty in Your Coffee Cup" <www.maketradefair.com/en/index.php?file= 16092002164814.htm>.

[7]Julie Grossman, "Mountain Groan," Resource Center of the Americas, January 2001 <www.organicconsumers.org/starbucks/fairtrade2.htm>.

[8]Oxfam International, "Mugged: Poverty in Your Coffee Cup."

[9]For further information on the effects of NAFTA on farmers, check out

Danny Duncan Collum, "One Side to Every Story," *Sojourners,* May 2007 <www.sojo.net/index.cfm?action=magazine.article&issue=soj07 05&article=070521>; and Elizabeth Palmberg, "World Market 101," *Sojourners,* May 2007 <www.sojo.net/index.cfm?action=magazine.article &issue=soj0705&article=070523>.

[10]Oxfam America, "Ten Reasons to Support Fair Trade," in "Just Add Justice: Bringing Fair Trade to Your Community" <www.oxfamamerica .org/whatwedo/campaigns/coffee/news_publications/justadd justice-1205.pdf>.

[11]David Kennedy, "Chiapas: Reflections on Trade, Immigration, and the Global Economy," Global Exchange site (September 28, 2008) <www .globalexchange.org/tours/ChiapasReflections.html>.

[12]"The Story," *Frontline World,* May 2003 <www.pbs.org/frontlineworld/ stories/guatemala.mexico/thestory.html>.

[13]Rebecca Meyer, "East Target," *The Daily Californian,* June 12, 2001 <www.dailycal.org:8080/article/5640/easy_target>.

[14]Chris Herlinger, "Cups of Cool Water in the Lethal Desert," *The Christian Century,* March 8, 2003 <http://findarticles.com/p/articles/mi_ m1058/is_5_120/ai_98754717>.

[15]Tamara Straus, "Fair Trade Coffee: Coming to a Café Near You," AlterNet, November 30, 2000 <www.alternet.org/story/10156/?page=entire>.

[16]In the United States TransfairUSA (www.transfairusa.org) provides such certification.

[17]Global Exchange site, "Fair Trade Coffee" (September 5, 2008) <www .globalexchange.org/campaigns/fairtrade/coffee/>.

[18]Go to their website at <www.tenthousandvillages.com>.

[19]Alex Renton, "This Is a Story About Gourmet Coffee and Genocide."

[20]Ibid.

[21]Robert Steinback, "A Just Strategy to Stem Illegal Immigration," Diogenes Media page (June 6, 2006) <www.robertsteinback.com/1242/2315 .html>.

[22]Find out more at <www.justcoffee.org>.

[23]For more information see <www.landof1000hills.com>.

[24]Erin Leigh, "When I Was Eight Years Old . . . ," Land of a Thousand Hills blog (December 2, 2008) <www.landof1000hills.com/ blog/?p=68>.

Chapter 2: Chocolate

[1]Gillonde, home page, "Tony and the Chocolate Factory Facts" (February 25, 2007) <http://gillonde.stumbleupon.com>. For more information see <www.chocolonely.nl>.

[2]For the sake of clarity, I've chosen to use the more traditional term *slave* instead of "people forced into slavery." I agree that a person's identity cannot be reduced to the label *slave*, but that term remains more commonly recognized.

[3]Lauren Comiteau, "Slaves to Chocolate?" *Time*, May 25, 2007 <www.time.com/time/magazine/article/0,9171,1625697,00.html?xid=rss-world>.

[4]Global Exchange site, "Facts About Fair Trade and the Cocoa Industry" (February 6, 2007) <www.globalexchange.org/campaigns/fairtrade/cocoa/facts.html>.

[5]Joël Glenn Brenner, *The Emperors of Chocolate: Inside the Secret World of Hershey and Mars* (New York: Random House, 1999), p. 232.

[6]Bureau of Democracy, Human Rights, and Labor, *U.S. State Department Report on Ivory Coast 2000*, February 23, 2001 <www.globalexchange.org/campaigns/fairtrade/cocoa/ussdIvoryCoast2000.pdf>.

[7]Global Exchange site, "The Chocolate Industry: Poverty Behind the Sweetness" (December 22, 2008) <www.globalexchange.org/campaigns/fairtrade/cocoa/background.html>.

[8]"Section 307 of the Smoot-Hawley Tariff Act of 1930 (19 U.S.C. 1307) states: 'All goods, wares, articles, and merchandise mined, produced, or manufactured wholly or in part in any foreign country by convict labor or forced labor . . . shall not be entitled to entry at any of the ports of the U.S., and the importation thereof is prohibited' " (Juliana Geron Pilon, "Tariff Act of 1930: Taking a Stand Against Slave Labor," *Issue Bulletin #102* [February 8, 1984] <www.heritage.org/research/tradeandeconomicfreedom/ib102.cfm>).

[9]Sudarsan Raghavan and Sumana Chatterjee, "Slave Labor Taints Sweetness of World's Chocolate," *Kansas City Star*, June 23, 2001 <www.globalexchange.org/campaigns/fairtrade/cocoa/kansascitystar062301.html>.

[10]Kevin Bales, *Disposable People: New Slavery in the Global Economy* (Berkeley: University of California Press, 1999), p. 8.

[11]This claim has basis in truth. In October 2008, U.S. Immigration and Customs Enforcement carried out a raid to arrest workers who had recently spoken up about being trafficked into the United States after Hurricane Katrina to work in forced labor camps. These victims were not only punished for speaking up but were also denied legal counsel (Saket Soni, "ICE Raid Targets, Snares Human Trafficking Victims," New Orleans' Workers Center for Racial Justice, October 29, 2008 <http://nolaworkerscenter.wordpress.com/2008/11/01/ice-raid-target-snares-victims-of-human-trafficking/>). Also in October of 2008, Operation Cross Country II targeted prostitutes in the United States, rescuing all trafficking victims under the age of eighteen but prosecuting all those over eighteen (Kevin Bohn, "Operation Frees Dozens of Child Prostitutes," CNN.com, October 27, 2008 <www.cnn.com/2008/CRIME/10/27/child.prostitutes.freed/index.html>).

[12]Keith Hopkins, *Conquerors and Slaves: Sociological Studies in Roman History* (Cambridge: Cambridge University Press, 1978), p. 102.

[13]I am indebted to Brian Walsh and Sylvia Keesmaat's fantastic book *Colossians Remixed: Subverting the Empire* (Downers Grove, Ill.: InterVarsity Press, 2004) for some of the ideas included in this section.

[14]The Hymns and Carols of Christmas page, "O Holy Night" <www.hymnsandcarolsofchristmas.com/Hymns_and_Carols/o_holy_night.htm>.

[15]Adolphe Adam, "O Holy Night," ca. 1847 <http://en.wikipedia.org/wiki/O_holy_night>.

[16]Stephen Tomkins, *William Wilberforce: A Biography* (Grand Rapids: Eerdmans, 2007), p. 50.

[17]Eric Metaxas, *Amazing Grace: William Wilberforce and the Heroic Campaign to End Slavery* (New York: HarperCollins, 2007), p. 63.

[18]Tomkins, pp. 67-68. These defenses of slavery in the nineteenth century are eerily similar to the excuses heard today to do nothing about modern-day slavery. They appeal to personal self-interest (safety, job security, economic stability) while feeding us the pseudolie that the slave would be worse off unemployed (as if the option of fairly compensated employment couldn't exist).

[19]Ibid., p. 213.

[20]William Hague, *William Wilberforce: The Life of the Great Anti-Slave*

Trade Campaigner (Orlando: Harcourt, 2007), p. 228.

[21]Tomkins, p. 218.

[22]Metaxas, p. xv.

[23]Global Exchange site, "The News on Chocolate Is Bittersweet: No Progress on Child Labor, but Fair Trade Chocolate Is on the Rise," June 2005 <www.globalexchange.org/campaigns/fairtrade/cocoa/chocolate report05.pdf>.

[24]Carol Off, *Bitter Chocolate: The Dark Side of the World's Most Seductive Sweet* (New York: The New Press, 2006), p. 143.

[25]"'Chocolate's Bittersweet Economy': Cocoa Industry Accused of Greed, Neglect for Labor Practices in Ivory Coast," *Democracy Now!* February 14, 2008 <www.democracynow.org/2008/2/14/chocolates_bittersweet _economy_cocoa_industry_accused>.

[26]*William Wilberforce Trafficking Victims Protection Reauthorization Act of 2007*, 110th Cong., H.R. 3887 <www.govtrack.us/congress/bill .xpd?bill=h110-3887>.

[27]Brenner, *Emperors of Chocolate*, p. 31.

[28]Stop the Traffik site, "Cocoa Industry Can't Guarantee Easter Without Slavery," press release, February 28, 2007 <www.stopthetraffik.org/ news/press/press280207.aspx>.

[29]Cadbury site, "Cadbury Dairy Milk Commits to Going Fairtrade," Cadbury Global, March 4, 2009 <www.cadbury.com/MEDIA/PRESS/Pages/ cdmfair trade.aspx>.

[30]Alexa Shaich, personal e-mail, "Re: Curious About the Benefit Dinner," April 24, 2008.

[31]See <www.ijm.org>. Also check out the Polaris Project <www.polaris project.org>.

[32]For more information, see <http://kiva.org>.

[33]Lauren Comiteau, "Slaves to Chocolate?"

Chapter 3: Cars

[1]Michael Hawthorne, "BP Dumps Mercury in Lake: Refinery Has Been Exempt—and New Permit Gives It 5 More Years," *Chicago Tribune,* July 27, 2007 <www.chicagotribune.com/services/newspaper/premium/ printedition/Friday/chi-mercury_27jul27,0,660106.story>.

[2]Antonia Juhasz, "Chevron's Hype," *Los Angeles Times,* November 21,

2008 <www.latimes.com/news/opinion/sunday/commentary/la-oe-juhasz21-2008nov21,0,4211763.story>; the commercials can be found (for now) at <www.chevron.com/about/advertising/>.

[3]Naomi Oreskes, "Beyond the Ivory Tower: The Scientific Consensus on Climate Change," *Science* 306, no. 5702 (2004), p. 1686 <www.sciencemag.org/cgi/content/full/306/5702/1686>. While scientific consensus is never an absolute guarantee, one cannot deny that scientists are currently in near-unanimous agreement that human-produced climate change is occurring. Those who continue to dispute this are usually lobbyists for some energy-industry-related interest group (like oil or car manufacturers) or else reporters seeking controversy.

[4]EcoBridge site, "Causes of Global Warming" <www.ecobridge.org/content/g_cse.htm>.

[5]Michael Jamison, "Warming Climate Shrinking Glacier Park's Glaciers," *USA Today,* October 15, 2007 <www.usatoday.com/weather/climate/globalwarming/2007-10-11-glacier-park_N.htm>.

[6]Jeremy Page, "Climate of Fear in Sinking Country," *Times* (U.K.), February 2, 2007 <www.commondreams.org/headlines07/0202-09.htm>.

[7]John Esterbrook, "U.S. Drowning Pacific Islands? Planned Lawsuit Says U.S., Australia Global Warming Sinking Islands," *CBS News,* April 28, 2002 <www.cbsnews.com/stories/2002/08/29/world/main520161.shtml>. Although proposed, the lawsuit stalled in early 2007. As of January 2009, the future of the lawsuit is unknown.

[8]Hawthorne, "BP Dumps Mercury in Lake."

[9]March of Dimes site, Pregnancy and Newborn Health Education Center page, "During Your Pregnancy: Things to Avoid" (July 2008) <www.marchofdimes.com/pnhec/159_15759.asp>.

[10]Michael Hawthorne, "BP Under Gun to Expand Production, Limit Pollution," *Chicago Tribune,* November 17, 2007 <www.chicagotribune.com/services/newspaper/printedition/monday/chi-bp_19nov19,0,7207099.story>.

[11]Unfortunately, a December 2008 court decided that, even though Chevron had hired and transported military forces, they would not be held responsible for the 1998 murders of protesters committed by their hired forces ("Chevron Cleared in 1998 Shooting Deaths of Protesters in Niger Delta," *Democracy Now!* site, December 2, 2008 <www

.democracynow.org/2008/12/2/chevron_cleared_in_1998_shooting
_deaths>).

[12]Emem J. Okon, "A Report of the Niger Delta Women for Justice (NDWJ)
on the Delta Women Siege on the American Oil Company, Chevron-
Texaco in Delta State of Nigeria" (August 2002) <www.ndwj.kabissa
.org/ArticlesResearch/DeltaWomenSeige/NDWomensSeige.pdf>.

[13]MisFortune 500 site, "Niger Delta Women Protest Against Chevron"
(July 2002) <www.misfortune500.org/Company/Show.aspx?articleid
=11>.

[14]Okon, "A Report of the Niger Delta Women for Justice."

[15]Niger Delta Women for Justice site, "Niger Women Protest Against
Chevron" (August 2002) <www.ndwj.kabissa.org/Escarvos_Protest/
escarvos_protest.html>.

[16]Ibid.

[17]Isioma Daniel, "Protests in the Nigerian Delta: Women's Tactics Stymie
Oil Grant," Ms. magazine (winter 2002) <www.msmagazine.com/
dec02/daniels.asp>.

[18]Kingsley Osadolor, "The Rise of the Women of the Niger Delta," World
Press Review 49, no. 10 (2002) <www.worldpress.org/Africa/725.cfm>.

[19]SNV Plastics site, "Global Warming on Plastic Bottles" <www.snv
plastics.com/articles/Global_warming_on_plastic_bottles.php>.

[20]Sustainable Table site, "Fossil Fuel and Energy Use".

[21]David Radcliff, e-mail to the author, "Re: Living Justly Questions," December 28, 2008.

[22]Joel Lovell, "Left-Hand-Turn Elimination," New York Times Magazine,
December 9, 2007 <www.nytimes.com/2007/12/09/magazine/09left-
handturn.html?_r=1>.

Chapter 4: Food

[1]Steven Greenhouse, "Tomato Pickers' Wages Fight Faces Obstacles,"
New York Times, December 24, 2007 <www.nytimes.com/2007/12/24/
us/24tomato.html?_r=2&adxnnl=1&oref=slogin&ref=us&adxnnlx
=1198515955b1azQbGU0aGlIvrfVbdwTw&oref=slogin>.

[2]Ibid.

[3]Coalition of Immokalee Workers site, "Guilty! On Eve of Trial, Farm

Bosses Plead Guilty to Enslaving Immokalee Workers in Tomato Harvest," August 13, 2008 <www.ciw-online.org/news.html>.

[4]Larry Lipman, "Sheriff: There Is Slavery in Florida Tomato Fields," *Palm Beach Post,* April 15, 2008 <www.palmbeachpost.com/state/content/state/epaper/2008/04/15/0415slavery.html>.

[5]Coalition of Immokalee Workers site, "Statement of Sen. Bernie Sanders on Slavery Verdict in Immokalee, Florida," September 3, 2008 <www.ciw-online.org/Sen_Sanders_on_Slavery_Verdict.html>.

[6]Associated Press, "McDonald's pays more for tomatoes, workers to benefit," *USA Today,* April 9, 2007 <www.usatoday.com/money/industries/food/2007-04-09-mcdonalds-tomatoes_N.htm>.

[7]Ibid.

[8]After the scare of mad cow disease, feeding cattle the remains of other cows was banned. But the chicken refuse the cows are fed contains leftover chicken feed (as well as their excrement), which typically contains cow remains.

[9]Other Western nations ban the use of such hormones, citing health and ethical concerns.

[10]"Livestock a Major Threat to Environment," Food and Agriculture Organization of the UN site, November 29, 2006 <www.fao.org/newsroom/en/news/2006/1000448/index.html>

[11]"How to Live Sustainably: An Interview with John Robbins," *Get Fresh!* (summer 2008) <www.fresh-network.com/acatalog/how-to-live-sustainably.html>.

[12]Food Reference site, "Cattle and Methane Gas," January 2006 <www.foodreference.com/html/a-cows-methane-815.html>.

[13]Tom Pelton, "Supergerms from Pigs and Chickens," *Baltimore Sun,* December 18, 2007 <http://weblogs.baltimoresun.com/news/local/bay_environment/blog/2007/12/supergerms_from_pigs_and_chick.html>.

[14]Peter Singer and Jim Mason, *The Ethics of What We Eat* (Emmaus, Penn.: Rodale, 2006), p. 63.

[15]Ibid., pp. 232-35.

[16]Wendell Berry, "Conservation Is Good Work," in *Sex, Economy, Freedom & Community* (New York: Pantheon Books, 1993), p. 34.

[17]Wendell Berry, "Christianity and the Survival of Creation," in *Sex, Economy, Freedom & Community* (New York: Pantheon Books, 1993), p.

98.

[18]J. Matthew Sleeth, *Serve God, Save the Planet* (Grand Rapids: Zondervan, 2007), p. 129.

[19]Josh Brown, personal e-mail, "Re: Organic Farming Interview?" May 21, 2008.

[20]Singer and Mason, *Ethics of What We Eat*, p. 221.

[21]Ibid., p. 42.

[22]For a fantastic collection of heirloom seeds visit <http://rareseeds.com>.

Chapter 5: Clothes

[1]Rachel Louise Snyder, *Fugitive Denim* (New York: W. W. Norton, 2008), p. 28.

[2]United Students Against Sweatsops, "Fair Labor Association Challenged Over Gildan Sweatshops," Jobs with Justice site <www.jwj.org/projects/slap/slactivist/2004winter.html>.

[3]Snyder, *Fugituve Denim*, p. 73.

[4]Marco Visscher, "Desperately Seeking Solutions: Why Are Indian Cotton Farmers Committing Suicide? And What Can Be Done to Help Them?" *Ode,* July/August 2006 <www.odemagazine.com/doc/35/desperately_seeking_solutions/>.

[5]Snyder, *Fugitive Denim*, p. 63.

[6]"ILO Warns on Farm Safety: Agriculture Mortality Rates Remain High, Pesticides Pose Major Health Risks to Global Workforce," International Labour Organization site, October 22, 1997 <www.ilo.org/global/About_the_ILO/Media_and_public_information/Press_releases/lang--en/WCMS_008027/index.htm>.

[7]"Endosulfan Deaths and Poisonings in Benin," *Pesticides News,* no. 47 (March 2000), pp. 12-14 <www.getipm.com/articles/benin-deaths.htm#Maregourou>.

[8]Snyder, *Fugitive Denim*, p. 136.

[9]"Children Exploited by Kathie Lee/Wal-Mart," The National Labor Committee site, April 29, 1996 <www.nlcnet.org/article.php?id=436>.

[10]Charles Kernaghan, "Child Labor Is Back: Children Are Again Sewing Clothing for Major U.S. Companies," The National Labor Committee site, October 2006 <www.nlcnet.org/admin/media/document/Report

PDF/Harvest_Rich/NLC_Child_Labor_WEB.pdf>.

[11]Charles Kernaghan, "Child Labor Is Back," The National Labor Committee site <www.nlcnet.org/article.php?id=147>.

[12]"Victoria's Secret Abuses Foreign Guest Workers in Jordan," The National Labor Committee site, November 26, 2007 <www.nlcnet.org/article.php?id=490>.

[13]James Geary and Marco Visscher, "New Model Army," *Ode Magazine* 6, no. 4 (2008): 54-63.

[14]For more information see <www.studentsagainstsweatshops.org>.

[15]Frederick Kopp, "Child Slave Labor in the Walt Disney Company," HIS Child Slave Labor site, November 2005 <http://ihscslnews.org/view_article.php?id=67>.

[16]Sarah Skidmore, "Nike Still Sees China Labor Challenges" <http://cbae.nmsu.edu/~dboje/nike/china.html>.

Chapter 6: Waste

[1]Kathy Marks and Daniel Howden, "The World's Rubbish Dump: A Garbage Tip that Stretches from Hawaii to Japan," *The Independent,* February 5, 2008 <www.independent.co.uk/environment/the-worlds-rubbish-dump-a-garbage-tip-that-stretches-from-hawaii-to-japan-778016.html>.

[2]Thomas Hayden, "Trashing Our Oceans: An Armada of Plastic Rides the Waves, and Sea Creatures Are Suffering," *U.S. News & World Report,* October 27, 2002 <www.usnews.com/usnews/culture/articles/021104/archive_023176.htm>.

[3]Elizabeth Royte, *Garbage Land: On the Secret Trail of Trash* (New York: Little, Brown and Company, 2005), p. 11.

[4]Ibid., p. 12.

[5]Hans Tammemagi, *The Waste Crisis: Landfills, Incinerators, and the Search for a Sustainable Future,* (New York: Oxford University Press, 1999), p. 8.

[6]Ibid., p. 9.

[7]Elizabeth Royte, *Garbage Land,* p. 165.

[8]Ibid., p. 166.

[9]Ibid., p. 169.

[10]Bryan Walsh, "The World's Most Polluted Places," *Time* <www.time

.com/time/specials/2007/article/0,28804,1661031_1661028
_1661020,00.html>.

[11]Jane McConnell, "The Joy of Cloth Diapers," *Mothering*, no. 88 (May/
June 1998) <www.mothering.com/articles/new_baby/diapers/joy-of-
cloth.html>.

[12]Ibid.

[13]Toxic shock syndrome is a potentially deadly infection caused by
toxic bacteria. The combination of high-absorbency tampons with
menstrual blood can be a ripe breeding ground for the bacteria. Reg-
ulating the chemicals in tampons has drastically reduced its
occurrence.

[14]For more information on cloth diapers, and for examples, check out
Better for Babies <http://betterforbabies.com>, The Diaper Pin <www
.diaperpin.com> and Nicki's Diapers <http://nickisdiapers.com>.

[15]Susan Strasser, *Waste and Want: A Social History of Trash* (New York:
Metropolitan Books, 1999), p. 163.

[16]For more information and product information check out GladRags
<www.gladrags.com> and Sckoon <http://sckoon.com>.

[17]Alecia Swasy, *Soap Opera: The Inside Story of Procter & Gamble* (New
York: Time Books, 1993), p. 158.

[18]Wendy Taylor, personal e-mail, "Re: Diaper Info," July 22, 2008.

[19]Miguel Llanos, "Plastic Bottles Pile Up as Mountains of Waste: Americans' Thirst for Portable Water Is Behind Drop in Recycling Rate,"
MSNBC.com, March 3, 2005 <www.msnbc.msn.com/id/5279230/>.

[20]For more information about composting visit <www.howtocompost
.org>.

[21]Paul Hawken, "Natural Capitalism: Resource Waste," *Mother Jones*,
March/April 1997 <www.motherjones.com/news/feature/1997/03/
hawken2.html>.

[22]See <http://plasticfree.blogspot.com/>.

[23]Robert D. McFadden and Angela Macropoulos, "Wal-Mart Employee
Trampled to Death," *New York Times*, November 29, 2008 <www
.nytimes.com/2008/11/29/business/29walmart.html>.

[24]After the terrorist attacks of 9/11, and again when faced with the mort-
gage crises of early 2008, President Bush encouraged the American
public to "go shopping more" as a way to stimulate our economy.

[25]Aldous Huxley, *Brave New World & Brave New World Revisited* (New York: Harper & Row, 1932), pp. 36-37.

[26]J. Matthew Sleeth, *Serve God, Save the Planet* (Grand Rapids: Zondervan, 2007), p. 18.

Chapter 7: Debt

[1]David Malin Roodman, *Still Waiting for the Jubilee: Pragmatic Solutions for the Third World Debt Crisis* (Washington, D.C.: Worldwatch Institute, 2001), p. 8.

[2]See <www.newlifeforhaiti.org>.

[3]Paul Farmer, *The Uses of Haiti* (Monroe, Maine: Common Courage Press, 2006), p. 56.

[4]Ibid., p. 67.

[5]Ibid., p. 85.

[6]Roodman, *Still Waiting for the Jubilee*, p. 20.

[7]"Beginners Guide to Debt: A Silent War," Jubilee USA Network <www.jubileeusa.org/resources/debt-resources/beginners-guide-to-debt/a-silent-war.html>.

[8]Roodman, *Still Waiting for the Jubilee*, p. 35.

[9]"Debt, the World Bank, the IMF and Water," Jubilee USA Network, February 9, 2007 <www.jubileeusa.org/fileadmin/user_upload/Resources/Policy_Archive/Debt_and_Water_2004.pdf>.

[10]Ibid.

[11]"The World Food Crisis," *New York Times,* editorial, April 10, 2008 <www.nytimes.com/2008/04/10/opinion/10thu1.html?scp=7&sq=haiti+food&st=nyt>.

[12]For further exploration of this connection see John Howard Yoder, *The Politics of Jesus* (Grand Rapids: Eerdmans, 1972).

[13]The Greek word used for debts here is *opheilema*, which elsewhere in Scripture (and in extrabiblical Greek texts) implies monetary debt. In the culture of Rome's oppressive taxation—and following the prayer's request for the food necessary for day-to-day survival—asking for monetary debts to be forgiven makes perfect sense.

[14]Roodman, *Still Waiting for the Jubilee*, p. 55.

[15]Desmond Tutu, "Debt Cancellation a Victory for the World," *Baltimore Sun*, May 7, 2008, A13.

[16]Jason Burke, "Mumbai: Behind the Attacks Lies a Story of Youth Twisted by Hate," *The Observer,* November 30, 2008 <www.guardian.co.uk/world/2008/nov/30/mumbai-terror-attacks-india>.

[17]In light of these situations, some have realized that it might be a better use of resources to, instead of bombing terrorists, start preventing the conditions that grow terrorists. Providing alternative schools that don't indoctrinate children to extremism is one such solution. Check out Greg Mortenson and David Oliver Relin's book *Three Cups of Tea* for a story of one man's mission to build schools in these impoverished regions of Pakistan. Similarly, Shaukat Ali, a former Taliban fighter who grew disillusioned with extremism, now devotes his time to setting up schools for girls in Kashmir. He believes children are the hope for the future, saying, "if they are educated, they can use dialogue and negotiation; they can distinguish between propaganda and reality. We are responsible for that before God" (Karin Ronnow, "The Transformation of an Extremist" *Ode Magazine,* November 2007 <www.odemagazine.com/doc/48/the-transformation-of-an-extremist/>).

[18]David Beckmann, "Jubilee Begins with Me," *Sojourners,* July/August 2000 <http:findarticlescom/p/articles/mi_qa3849/is_200007/ai_n8909560>.

Conclusion

[1]A term generally attributed to Dr. Cornel West.

[2]*The Colbert Report,* Comedy Central, April 4, 2008.

[3]Richard Foster, *Celebration of Discipline* (San Francisco: HarperSanFrancisco, 1988), p. 87.

[4]Pirkei Avos, Chapter 2, Mishna 21 <www.torah.org/learning/pirkeiavos/chapter2-21.html>. The Talmud is a collection of ancient rabbinic sayings that serves to educate and guide Jewish people, in addition to the Torah.

About the Author

Julie Clawson is a mom, writer, and former pastor who is simply trying to figure out how she can love God and others every day. Not that it's easy, or that she does it all that well, but she does her best knowing that it will be a lifelong journey.

Julie grew up as a follower of Christ. She graduated from Wheaton College in Wheaton, Illinois, where she also earned a graduate degree in intercultural studies. She then spent over a decade serving in churches in the Chicago suburbs, but now lives in Austin, Texas, with her family. With her husband, Mike, and two kids, Emma and Aidan, Julie enjoys Austin's ecoconscious culture and visits the farmers' market regularly.

Julie spends way too much time online, but appreciates the community she has discovered there. She moderates the Emerging Women (emerging women.us) and Emerging Parents (emergingparents.com) blogs and loves learning from others who are exploring how to practically live out their faith. When her kids give her a few minutes to relax, Julie enjoys meeting friends for a good cup of (fair-trade) coffee, discussing theology, playing strategy board games, attending Renaissance Faires (in costume), working in her garden and reading fantasy novels.

Julie is grateful for this opportunity to share what she has learned about seeking everyday justice, and would love to continue the discussion and learn from all the readers of this book. She invites you to visit her blog (julieclawson.com) and the Everyday Justice site (everydayjus tice.net) to join the conversation, discover more about justice issues and find out about justice-related events in your area. In addition, if you would like Julie to speak at your event or gathering, or simply have any questions about the book, please contact her at julie@everydayjus tice.net.

LIKEWISE. *Go and do.*

A man comes across an ancient enemy, beaten and left for dead. He lifts the wounded man onto the back of a donkey and takes him to an inn to tend to the man's recovery. Jesus tells this story and instructs those who are listening to "go and do likewise."

Likewise books explore a compassionate, active faith lived out in real time. When we're skeptical about the status quo, Likewise books challenge us to create culture responsibly. When we're confused about who we are and what we're supposed to be doing, Likewise books help us listen for God's voice. When we're discouraged by the troubled world we've inherited, Likewise books encourage us to hold onto hope.

In this life we will face challenges that demand our response. Likewise books face those challenges with us so we can act on faith.

likewisebooks.com